MW00910348

GOD101

A Deep Well of Wisdom

Kurt Langstraat was born to be a pastor. Many lives have been enriched by Kurt's passion to see people grow in their relationship with Christ. His blend of natural pastoral gifts, years of proven leadership, and genuine love for people is evident to all.

As you read through Kurt's thoughts on the Book of John, you will glean treasures from a man who has spent much time learning about God. More importantly, you will be impacted by the heart of a worshiper who has consistently lingered in the life-molding presence of God. Kurt provides a deep well of wisdom for those thirsty for more of Jesus.

~ **Marty Nystrom**; author, songwriter, recording artist, worship leader, teacher

Discover Hidden Treasures

You will enjoy the insight and devotion presented by Kurt in this book. He and Gwen have been terrific parents, and their children are living proof of their commitment. Please read, enjoy and grow as you discover the treasures hidden within these pages.

~ **Betsey Hayford;** Pastor, *International Church of Foursquare Gospel*

Have Your Faith Built and Your Understanding Increased

You will love reading Kurt's rich insights from God's Word. His writing combines a real love for Jesus Christ plus years of pastoral experience. He has counseled hundreds of people through many differing kinds of problems, and has seen what the power of the Holy Spirit can do. Get ready to have your faith built up and your understanding increased!

~ **Dr. Kim Ryan;** Lead Pastor, *North County Christ the King Church,* Lynden, Washington

Deep, Honest, Creative

I have known Kurt Langstraat for many years, so the depth, honesty and creativity of these reflections on the Book of John are not surprising. This beautiful compilation will be meaningful to new believers in Jesus Christ, insightful to those who are searching for Him, and as a practical means of building successful mentoring relationships.

~ **Timothy Salzman;** Professor of Music, *University of Washington*

GOD101

GOD101

GOD101

Getting to Know God

Kurt Langstraat

GOD101

Kurt Langstraat

With Jeanne Halsey

Second Edition
ISBN 978-1-105-12563-8

For more information, contact:

Kurt Langstraat

North County Christ the King

1816 - 18th Street

Lynden, Washington 98264

United States of America

360.318.9446

klangstraat@hotmail.com

www.ncctk.com

GOD101

Table of Contents

GOD101

Introduction

GOD101 is for anyone who wants to know God.

The way to get to know God is by reading about Him in the Bible. A great place to start is in the Book of John.

The Book (or Gospel) of John was written by one of Jesus' disciples whose name is John. It is named after him because it is his account of the time he spent with Jesus, what he saw Jesus do, what he heard Jesus say, and Who he believes Jesus is. John was very close to Jesus; in fact, he referred to himself as *"the one Jesus loved."*

I am deeply indebted to **Dr. Warren W. Wiersbe,** for insights and quotations from his *The Bible Exposition Commentary.*

My prayer is that *GOD101* will display Jesus Christ, the Son of God, in all His glory, power, kindness, humor, reality, and – above all – His eternal love.

Day 1: *"In the Beginning"*

John 1:1-5

The Word is the Creator of the World

Everything has a beginning, right? You do, I do. You began when you were conceived by your mother and father. Jesus also had a beginning as a human when Mary became pregnant by the power of God. We call it the "immaculate conception."

Most people think Jesus began at Christmas, when He was born a human baby and laid in a manger. But in fact, Jesus did not begin there. Jesus did not "begin" at all. He is **eternal.**

He has always existed, along with God the Father and God the Holy Spirit. I will not pretend to understand the Triune Nature of God, but as we begin our study of God, it is important to understand that Jesus existed as God before He took on human form. John begins his account of Jesus at the creation of the world:

> In the beginning, the Word already existed. The Word was with God, and the Word was God.
>
> **John 1:1**

This "Word" John talks about is Jesus, as you will find in the verses that follow. It is important to know this starting out, because John makes it clear that Jesus is God. He existed before He became a man. He existed with God. He is God. This is an important verse to refer to when the two guys on bikes come knocking on your door.

> He existed in the beginning with God. God created everything through Him, and nothing was created except through Him.
>
> **John 1:2-3**

Again, John makes it clear that Jesus did not begin as a baby – He existed as God before He was born as a human. Before the Universe was created, before the Earth was made, before the first man, in eternity past, Jesus existed as fully God ... before He got a "bod."

Then John tells that Jesus was actually the One Who created everything. So not only did He exist as God before the beginning of Time, but He was the One responsible for creating all we see. Awesome. Not just a baby in a manger. Not just a great teacher. Not just a man hanging on a cross. But God, the Creator of EVERYTHING! That's Jesus.

> The Word gave life to everything that was created, and His life brought light to everyone. The light shines in the darkness, and the darkness can never extinguish it.
>
> **John 1:4-5**

Now John tells us that Jesus created everything, and then gave life to everything He created. He is the One responsible for us coming to life, having life. So of course it makes sense that He is the **Way** to Eternal Life. Since it all began with Him, of course, Eternal Life would happen through Him. His life is the light we all need to find our way to God.

This world would be dark and hopeless without Jesus, but He is here ... and He is Light, and He brings light and hope to everyone. Life may seem dark, sometimes, but with Jesus in your life, there is always hope, always light, you always know where you are going.

That's probably enough for one day. Did you learn anything new about God?

Day 2: John the B

John 1:6-14

The Eternal Jesus Comes As the Father's Son

What is your nickname? When I was a kid, my friend Freddy used to call me "Kurt Ostrich" because I was tall and skinny, and I walked with a forward lunge, leading with my head. I didn't like that nickname very much.

John now begins to tell us about another John – John the Baptist – who was born just before Jesus. Can you guess why he was called "the Baptist"? If you remember, John the Baptist was the one who told everyone to repent because the Kingdom of God (Jesus) was near.

> God sent a man, John the Baptist, to tell about the Light, so that everyone might believe because of his testimony. John himself was not the Light; he was simply a witness to tell about the Light. The one who is the True Light, Who gives light to everyone, was coming into the world.
>
> **John 1:6-9**

John the Baptist was born to Elizabeth, who was Mary's cousin. When Mary was pregnant with Jesus, she went to visit Elizabeth ... and John (the Baptist) was the baby in Elizabeth's womb who jumped inside of her when Mary came near.

John the Baptist went out preaching and baptizing people, and he even baptized Jesus. John was telling people about Jesus, the Light Who was coming.

> He came into the very world He created, but the world didn't recognize Him. He came to His own people, and even they rejected Him.
>
> **John 1:10-11**

Think about this: Jesus creates this world and gives life to Mankind, and then He comes to the people He created. And they don't accept Him. They turn Him away. They reject Him. They eventually will kill Him. One might think God had failed. But actually, this is all a part of God's plan to call His Creation back to Himself, the plan that was formed **before** the Earth was formed – the plan called "redemption."

> But to all who believed Him and accepted Him, He gave the right to become children of God. They are reborn - not with a physical birth resulting from human passion or plan, but a birth that comes from God.
>
> **John 1:12-13**

This is the most amazing thing of all! If we believe in what John is telling us, if we accept that Jesus is God, then we become God's own children. Awesome. Simply incredible. In fact,

John tells us that if we accept by faith that this is true, then we are reborn into a spiritually awakened person, connected to God through Jesus.

> So the Word became human and made His home among us. He was full of unfailing love and faithfulness. And we have seen His glory, the glory of the Father's one and only Son.
>
> **John 1:14**

John sums it up for us: Jesus – eternal God, alive with the Father and the Spirit for Eternity past – becomes human. He enters this world through the birth canal of a young woman named Mary. He is ***"God in a bod":*** God in the form of a human, *"Emmanuel, God with us."* He came to live, to love, to die, and to save. Because He allowed Himself to be born into this world, He is called *"the Son of God."*

Day 3: Eternal God

John 1:14-18

Eternity Into Humanity

Have you ever tried to really think about Eternity? Someone being Eternal, no beginning and no end? My head hurts when I try to think about Eternity. We cannot understand it because Time and Space are normal to us. Eternity is God's normal.

> So the Word became human and made His home among us. He was full of unfailing love and faithfulness. And we have seen His glory, the glory of the Father's one and only Son.
>
> **John 1:14**

Remember that Jesus is called the Word because He is fully the expression and the revelation of the eternal God, born as a human baby. Born to be one of His own creation. That happened through His miraculous conception in a young Jewish woman named Mary, who gave birth to this Word-Child – fully God, fully divine, yet bound by the same human limitations as each of us. He would face the same temptations and work through the same feelings as we each do. He would have the same human tendencies and frailties we each have. However, every decision He made, He would make in perfect love and in faithfulness to what His Heavenly Father wanted

Him to do. He would live a perfect life without ever sinning.

Today, no matter what you are facing, Jesus knows, He understands and He cares deeply for you. Whether you are experiencing loneliness, disappointment, stress, or sickness – Jesus cares. Perhaps you are afraid of losing someone, perhaps even your life is threatened by cancer or some other disease – Jesus wants to enter your pain and share it with you. Maybe you have been abandoned, or someone has broken your heart, or even broken their covenant vows with you – Jesus is here for you, right here, right now. He wants to comfort you. Maybe you are afraid because you don't know what the future holds for you – Jesus knows, so the best thing you could do is get to know the One Who knows.

John tells us that the Jesus whom His friends knew and lived with for over three years was glorious. The glory of Heaven poured out of Him, He brought Heaven to Earth. He was perfect, He had power over the wind and the sea, over sickness and disease, over Satan and his demons, over death – and ultimately, over life. The glory of God raised Him from the dead as the first Eternal Man, leading the way and making a way for each of us. That is glorious!

> John testified about Him when he shouted to the crowds, "This is the One I was talking about when I said, 'Someone is coming after me Who is far greater

> than I am, for He existed long before me.'"
>
> **John 1:15**

Again, John tells us that John the Baptist confirmed that Jesus is the eternal God when he said that Jesus had existed long before he had. You see, John the Baptist was born before Jesus was, but he points out that Jesus is God – and so He was fully alive, as God, long before He ever arrived on this Earth as a baby. Eternal God coming to reveal Himself to the very ones He created.

> From His abundance we have all received one gracious blessing after another. For the law was given through Moses, but God's unfailing love and faithfulness came through Jesus Christ. No one has ever seen God. But the unique One, Who Himself is God, is near to the Father's heart. He has revealed God to us.
>
> **John 1:16-18**

Here John assures us that Jesus didn't come to judge us, but to live for us, die for the forgiveness of our sins, and to be raised with the first Eternal Body of many who would follow, all who receive His grace. Jesus is our Prototype, we will be like Him when we receive our new bodies.

These are some of the gracious blessings John is referring to. He reminds the Jews (and us) that Moses brought the Law to them. The Law is like a school teacher: they are there to define what you need to know, and to correct you when you are wrong. That's the purpose of the Law, the Ten Commandments. It defines how we are to live, and corrects us when we live wrongly.

But the Law does not give Eternal Life; only Jesus does. That is what John the Baptist was telling the people. He was telling them change was coming, that the Law was not enough to save them ... and Jesus Christ was now here – not to replace the Law – but to give them a better reason to want to keep the Law: LOVE. Jesus was here to LOVE and forgive them.

Then John again tells us that although no one has ever seen God – because He is invisible, He is spirit – Jesus is God revealed to us in a way that they were honored to see and understand, touch and feel, hug and hold, hear and observe. Jesus – even though He left His glorious eternal position and confined Himself to the limitations of a human body – was still connected to the mind and heart of God. He gave us an accurate expression of God's heart for us. His compassion for drunks and prostitutes, His anger toward hypocrisy, His heart for the hurting, His desire to heal those who desperately needed His touch.

He has not changed. This is still true today:

Jesus loves us, this we know
For the Bible tells us so.

Day 4: A Voice in the Wilderness

John 1:19-28

John the B Knows His Purpose

Do you know who you are and what is your purpose in Life? God made you on purpose, for a purpose. It is so great to find out who you are, and to let God use your unique gifts, abilities and passions to help build His Kingdom. John the B knew God's purpose for his life, and he lived it completely.

> This was John's testimony when the Jewish leaders sent priests and Temple assistants from Jerusalem to ask Him, "Who are you?"
>
> He came right out and said, "I am not the Messiah."
>
> "Well, then, who are you?" they asked. "Are you Elijah?"
>
> "No," he replied.
>
> "Are you the Prophet we are expecting?"
>
> "No."

> "Then who are you? We need an answer for those who sent us. What do you have
>
> to say about yourself?"

John 1:19-22

Here John – Jesus' friend and follower – is talking about John the Baptist, who was sent by God to prepare the Jews for Jesus. He preached for them to turn from sin and receive the Kingdom of God. The Jewish leaders were not sure who John the B was, so in this passage they were questioning him. They thought he might be the great prophet Elijah come back from the dead.

This tells us that John the B had a pretty powerful and radical ministry if the Jews thought he might be one of their most famous prophets. They really wanted to know who he was because he was upsetting their little balanced religious world, and they wanted some answers. This seems to be an ongoing theme with God: He is committed to shaking up religiosity and the status quo.

> John replied in the words of the prophet Isaiah: "I am a voice shouting in the wilderness, 'Clear the way for the Lord's coming!'"

John 1:23

Here John the B minimizes himself to focus all attention on Jesus Christ. This is what a true worshiper does: at all times, they keep the focus on Jesus. John the B says, "I am nothing more than a voice, a voice to inspire and exhort you, that there is change coming. Get ready, God has come to Earth."

> Then the Pharisees who had been sent asked him, "If you aren't the Messiah or Elijah or the Prophet, what right do you have to baptize?"
>
> John told them, "I baptize with water, but right here in the crowd is Someone you do not recognize. Though His ministry follows mine, I am not even worthy to be His slave and untie the straps of His sandal." This encounter took place in Bethany, an area east of the Jordan River, where John was baptizing.
>
> **John 1:24-28**

They did not get it, so now the Jewish leaders are asking for more information. They wanted to know why he was baptizing because baptism to them signified being indoctrinated into a belief system or a sect. The Jews baptized Gentiles who wanted to join the Jewish faith. John was baptizing Jews, so the leaders were probably worried he was stealing their people.

Normally a man like John would need to be commissioned by "someone important" (or qualified) to baptize, so they were really asking who gave him the right. The truth was, John had been commissioned by God Himself to baptize people, not to join a sect but as an expression of their repentance. He would preach, they would repent from their sin, and he would baptize them as an expression of their repentance.

Then John again does what he was designed to do. Instead of keeping the significance of his ministry for himself, he pointed the leaders to Jesus. This time he affirms that Jesus is in the crowd, and that He is the reason for all John is doing.

True worship has to do with deflecting all our success, all our significance, all our accomplishment, all our self, to the One Who lives in us and enables us: Jesus Christ. True worship recognizes that were it not for our Savior, there would be no purpose to anything we do. All of it will pass away one day – except the motivation for **being** who we are and **doing** what we do. That motivation is gratitude for being loved when we do not deserve it, which results in the desire to bring glory and attention to Jesus Christ. That has a lasting quality which will go on for eternity. That is worship.

Day 5: The Lamb

John 1:28-34

John the B Identifies Jesus

I love lambs. They are cute and fuzzy and soft. When we attend the County Fair, we always go to the sheep barn to see if there are any newly-born lambs. If we are lucky, we get to pet them.

> The next day, John saw Jesus coming toward him, and said, "Look! The Lamb of God Who takes away the sin of the world! He is the One I was talking about when I said, 'A Man is coming after me Who is far greater than I am, for He existed long before me.'"
>
> **John 1:28-30**

"Lamb" – isn't that an interesting name to call the Creator of the Universe? A lamb? But not just any lamb – the Lamb of God Who takes away the sin of the world. Every Jew who heard John the Baptist call Jesus a lamb knew the significance of this name.

The people of Israel were familiar with lambs for their sacrifices. At Passover, each family had to have a sacrificial lamb; and during the year, two lambs a day were sacrificed at the temple altar; plus all the other lambs brought for personal sacrifices. Those lambs were brought ***by men to men*** – but here is Jesus, God's Lamb, ***given by***

God to men! Those lambs could not take away sin, but the Lamb of God, Jesus, would take away all sin for all time. Those lambs were for Israel alone, but this Lamb would shed His blood for the whole world! He shed His blood for you.

> "I did not recognize Him as the Messiah, but I have been baptizing with water so that He might be revealed to Israel."
>
> **John 1:31**

Baptism was a foreshadowing of what Jesus the Lamb of God would endure for the sins of the world. He would submit Himself to a man, John the Baptist, to put Him down under the water, fully dead to self, and rise up full of the Holy Spirit and the power to complete the work before Him. Jesus would submit himself to the hands of men, to be put on a cross, put into a tomb, and in three days, raise in the power of God, completing the work of defeating Death and Hell on the cross.

Jesus' baptism was very significant, and so is ours. Jesus was showing His world what He would do to save the world. When we get baptized, we are showing our world that we are dying to our old nature, our old patterns of living and relating, and rising up out of the water to a new life, new ways, following Jesus all the way to Heaven.

> Then John testified, "I saw the Holy Spirit descending like a dove from Heaven and resting upon Him. I didn't

> know He was the One, but when God sent me to baptize with water, He told me, 'This One on Whom you see the Spirit descend and rest is the One Who will baptize with the Holy Spirit.' I saw this happen to Jesus, so I testify that He is the Chosen One of God.
>
> **John 1:32-34**

Something different happened when John the Baptist baptized Jesus. The Holy Spirit – Who is the part of God Who speaks to us and lives in us when we receive Jesus – identified Jesus to John and to all who were standing there. The Holy Spirit had prepared John the B for this moment by telling him that as he baptized people, there would be ONE Who would come to him Who would be different from all the rest.

The Holy Spirit told John the B he would see the Spirit coming down and resting upon this ONE. Sure enough, as John baptized Jesus, he saw the Spirit coming down and resting on Him. And so John concurs with all the rest of the witnesses, that Jesus truly is God. This ONE, Jesus Christ, would lead the way for all who believe in Him to have their sins forgiven and be filled with God's Holy Spirit too. It is the Holy Spirit in us that empowers us to become more and more like Jesus in our character, and to live a life that is more and more pleasing to God.

Day 6: The One

John 1:35-44

The One You Don't Want to Miss!

When I first started dating the woman who became my wife, it was not very long before I knew she was the ONE. She was cute, fun and intelligent, and we loved hanging out together. I am so glad she said YES to me because it would have been really disappointing to miss the ONE!

In John 1:35-44, John is still writing about John the Baptist, and how his preaching and baptizing prepared the way for Jesus to enter and begin HIs public ministry as Messiah, the ONE Who comes to save.

> The following day, John was again standing with two of his disciples. As Jesus walked by, John looked at Him and declared, "Look! There is the Lamb of God!" When John's two disciples heard this, they followed Jesus.
>
> Jesus looked around and saw them following. "What do you want?" He asked them.
>
> They replied, "Rabbi (which means 'Teacher), where are You staying?"

> "Come and see," He said. It was about four o'clock in the afternoon when they went with Him to the place where He was staying, and they remained with Him the rest of the day.
>
> **John 1:35-39**

This is where John the Baptist quietly leaves the stage of our study. He has done his part, he has prepared the way for God to come and be revealed, he has done what God called him to do. He will continue preaching, but we'll not hear much more of him until he loses his head for standing up for God and His Word. It is worth noting that the last thing we hear him say is, *"Look, there's God!"* – which results in two of his best men leaving him to follow Jesus. John the B's slogan regarding Jesus Christ was: ***"I must decrease so He (the ONE) may increase"*** (John 3:30). Wouldn't that be a great slogan by which to live our lives?

John's two disciples follow Jesus, and He invites them over to hang out and talk. We don't get to hear much of the conversation, but I would imagine spending the whole day with Jesus would evoke some pretty amazing conversations. They were convinced, and followed Him the rest of His life on Earth.

> Andrew, Simon Peter's brother, was one of these men who heard what John said and then followed Jesus. Andrew went to find his brother, Simon, and told him,

"We have found the Messiah" (which means 'Christ'). Then Andrew brought Simon to meet Jesus.
Looking intently at Simon, Jesus said, "Your name is Simon, son of John - but you will be called Cephas" (which means 'Peter'). The next day, Jesus decided to go to Galilee. He found Philip and said to him, "Come, follow Me." Philip was from Bethsaida, Andrew and Peter's hometown.

John 1:40-44

These men were real, they had real names. Andrew was the name of one of them. It is important as we think of them to remember they had names, faces, lives, jobs, and families. They had parents, friends and relatives who were important to them. What would it be like if Jesus showed up in your life – right where you are at – and invited you to give Him the entire next three years of your life? To leave school, leave a job, leave your home, leave your friends? The point is clear – all these things can be returned to – but this was the chance of a lifetime: to follow Jesus!

That chance still exists today. When you decide to follow Jesus, He is likely to give you new dreams, new desires, new hopes, and a new future. It is wonderful! It is the most exciting and significant ride on this planet. And you get to impact people's lives for eternity. You get to say, *"I had a part in that person coming to Christ"* or *"I am helping him grow as a Christian"* or *"She is being baptized because I showed her the way."* There is nothing more significant than having a part in where people spend Eternity, and in their lives changing for the better.

It is also important to remember you don't have to be a Peter, Paul or Mary to have great significance. Andrew didn't write any part of the Bible ... but he was the one who brought his brother Simon to Jesus. Jesus promptly gave Simon a new name, "Peter," which means "the Rock" – and a star was born!

The point is this: perhaps the most meaningful thing you could do for Jesus is simply be an influence. Influence means "to flow into." Flow into your family for Jesus. Flow into the people you work with for Jesus. Flow into every circumstance you are involved with for Jesus. Flow into the people you live with for Jesus. Who knows: someone you "flow into" for Jesus might be the next "Rock" in the Kingdom.

Day 7: A Hand-Picked Team

John 1:43-51

Jesus is Choosing People to Follow Him

When I was a kid, on warm Spring days after school, the neighborhood boys and girls would meet at the empty lot near our house, and we would play softball. The best players would be the captains and they would pick their teams. I always feared being picked last, especially after the last girl had been picked. *"We'll take Colleen – you can have Kurt."* Ouch!

> The next day, Jesus decided to go to Galilee. He found Philip and said to him, "Come, follow Me." Philip was from Bethsaida, Andrew and Peter's hometown.
>
> Philip went to look for Nathanael, and told him, "We have found the very person Moses and the prophets wrote about! His Name is Jesus, the Son of Joseph from Nazareth."
>
> "Nazareth!" exclaimed Nathanael. "Can anything good come from Nazareth?"
>
> "Come and see for yourself," Philip replied.

John 1:43-46

None of this is random. Jesus knows whom He wants on His team, and He goes out to find them. God still pursues people today, and He is pursuing you. He wants your heart, and wants you to get to know Him, to trust Him and follow Him.

Philip trusted Jesus so much that he immediately went and found his friend Nathanael, to tell him that the Messiah, the Savior, had come – and they had found Him: Jesus of Nazareth! Nathanael was not so easily convinced, and apparently didn't have such a good opinion of Nazareth, Jesus' home town. Nazareth was like the wrong side of the tracks, and if Jesus was from there, Nathanael had already formed his opinion about Him. We never do that, do we?

Philip simply invited him to *"Come and see."* He was saying, *"Don't take my word for it, discover for yourself that God is real and wants to know you."*

> As they approached, Jesus said, "Now here is a genuine son of Israel – a man of complete integrity."
>
> **John 1:47**

When Philip and Nathanael approach, Jesus has a little fun with Nathanael. He uses this phrase *"complete integrity"* (or "without guile") to describe Nathanael. Every Jew knew that guile was a common reference to Jacob, their forefather. Jacob was known to be deceptive, who had wrestled with the God-man in Genesis 32 and lost. Jacob had walked with a limp ever since.

Many theologians believe that this God-man was none other than God pre-incarnate, Jesus Christ. Isn't it ironic that the very Jesus talking to Nathanael about his ancestor Jacob, was the same Christ now incarnate (in a bod) Who had wrestled with Jacob hundreds of years previously.

Guile means to have ill intentions, ill motives in your heart. Being God, Jesus already knows Nathanael's opinion of Him, so He just played with him a little. You know how it feels when you say something about someone, and they overhear you by mistake? That's how Nathanael might have felt about his comment about the people from Nazareth. Jesus lets him have a little glimpse of the "inside information" He has about him. And it worked, because Nathanael seemed surprised and perhaps even uncomfortable with what Jesus knew about him.

> "How do You know about me?" Nathanael asked.
>
> Jesus replied, "I could see you under the fig tree before Philip found you."
>
> Then Nathanael exclaimed, "Rabbi, You are the Son of God – the King of Israel!"
>
> **John 1:48-49**

My take on it? I think Jesus knew things about

Nathanael was that Nate didn't want Jesus to know, and Jesus was using a little sarcasm of His own by comparing Nathanael to the deceiver Jacob. Nathanael, surprised, asks Jesus how He knows about him, and Jesus tells him he saw him under the fig tree.

The question I have is: what do you suppose Nathanael was doing under the fig tree? Whatever he was doing – whether it was napping, eating, looking at porn on his wireless, or praying – Jesus saw him and told him He saw him.

Apparently, Nathanael realizes the only way Jesus could have seen him is supernaturally, so he quickly taps out. He doesn't ask Jesus, "So, what else do you know about me?" – but ends the conversation with the confession, "Okay, okay, I believe, you are the Son of God!" Jesus had compared Nathanael to Jacob in His first comment about him, and Nathanael, being a good Jew, had not missed the comparison.

> Jesus asked him, "Do you believe this just because I told you I had seen you under the fig tree? You will see greater things than this." Then He said, "I tell you the truth: you will all see Heaven open and the angels of God going up and down on the Son of Man, the One Who is the stairway between Heaven and Earth."
>
> **John 1:50-51**

Jesus pulls Nate in a little more by telling him, "This is nothing! You come with Me, and you will see things that will blow your mind. You will see Heaven open up, and you will see angels coming and going upon Me – for I am the Way, the Stairway between Heaven and Earth." Jesus is the Stairway to Heaven. (Sorry, *Led Zep,* He can't be bought.) You want to get to Heaven, you have to take the Stairway, which is Jesus.

Here Jesus is again referencing a story about Jacob, this time the account from Genesis 28. Jacob had seen a stairway coming down out of Heaven, with angels going up and down the stairway; this is the place where God had blessed him. The point is this: you cannot hide from God. He sees, He knows, and He will confront and pursue you to call you into a meaningful life of integrity.

Integrity means basically that you live an undivided life for God, that you keep your heart pure, that your private life is congruous with your public expression of living. If you follow Him, take the Stairway. God will bless you like he blessed Jacob. Jesus called out Nathanael to live a life of integrity, and He is still calling us out today.

Day 8: First Miracle

John 2:1-12

Jesus Performs His First (Recorded) Miracle

Have you ever witnessed a real miracle? I have. Well, really, it was a healing. On a Thursday afternoon, I witnessed a girl named Heather Craker be healed instantly of a tumor behind her eye, in her brain. The tumor had been unmistakably visible on a previous MRI, so she was scheduled for surgery on Friday, which was the next day.

A bunch of people gathered and prayed for her just before she went in to the hospital for pre-surgery imaging. They took the pictures ... and the tumor was gone! Instead of having surgery on that Friday, she ran in the Track Meet at school that afternoon.

In John 2, Jesus performs His first miracle that is recorded.

> The next day, there was a wedding celebration in the village of Cana in Galilee. Jesus' mother was there, and Jesus and His disciples were also invited to the celebration. The wine supply ran out during the festivities, so Jesus'

mother told Him, "They have no more wine."

"Dear woman, that's not our problem," Jesus replied. "My time has not yet come."

But His mother told the servants, "Do whatever He tells you."

John 2:1-5

Jewish weddings lasted seven days. People would stay at the family's home, and the family would be expected to feed their guests for the entire seven days. Weddings were a time of great joy and celebration, and it would have been disappointing and shaming to the family to run out of food or wine for their guests. Mary probably didn't expect a miracle out of Jesus; He was the oldest son, so with her husband Joseph (presumably) dead, it was normal for her to turn to Him for help.

Jesus reminds her that He is on His Heavenly Father's timetable now, as He had done in the temple when He was 12 years old. Remember the time His parents lost track of Him, and when they finally found Him back at the temple, He told them, *"Not to worry, I have been busy doing My Father's business."* But as a good mom can, Mary uses her influence and tells the servants to cooperate with Jesus.

Or perhaps during His childhood, young Jesus was always performing little miracles around the house? Causing the wheat to grow despite a drought? Resurrecting the dead cat that was run over by a wagon? Healing His little brother's broken leg? Who knows?

> Standing nearby were six stone water jars, used for Jewish ceremonial washing. Each could hold 20 to 30 gallons. Jesus told the servants, "Fill the jars with water." When the jars had been filled, He said, "Now dip some out, and take it to the master of ceremonies." So the servants followed His instructions.
>
> **John 2:-6-8**

Jesus' miracles nearly always served the purpose of teaching or revealing something about God. Remember that Moses' first miracle was a plague of turning water into blood, which was about God's judgment against the people of Egypt. Here we have Jesus turning water into wine, a miracle of grace to bring joy to a wedding.

Wine symbolized joy in the Jewish tradition, and the lesson is clear. The world is very limited in the joy it can offer and, in fact, runs out very quickly. The right thing to do is turn to the Joy-Giver, the Wine-Maker, and let Him fill you when you have come to the end of your resources.

Why a wedding? Marriage is one of the clearest pictures of our relationship to Jesus Christ as His Church. In Ephesians 5, Paul tells us marriage is an illustration of how corporately – all of us believers– as one belong to Jesus, that we are His Bride. He loves and cares for us as a good, loving Husband would care for His Bride. Jesus will present us to the Father, a perfect Bride, without blemish, because of His forgiveness of our sins, made possible by the Wine of His Blood that would be poured out for us. So the imagery of this first miracle is very powerful and very fitting for Jesus' first public miracle.

> When the master of ceremonies tasted the water that was now wine, not knowing where it had come from (though of course the servants knew), he called the bridegroom over. "A host always serves the best wine first," he said. "Then when everyone has had a lot to drink, he brings out the less expensive wines. But you have kept the best until now!"
>
> **John 2:9-10**

Jesus' wine was amazing, far better than the first wine that was served. At a party, the best wine gets served first while the palate is still fresh and before the senses are numbed. You know how it is: after a couple of glasses, it doesn't matter so much anymore how good the wine is. The point is: what Jesus offers us in the way of joy is far better than anything the world can offer.

And notice He did not fill the 20-gallon stone jars with wine to sit and go bad. No, they were filled with water – and only what was dipped out was consumed by the wedding guests. This is to show that Jesus' joy is fresh and new every time you dip into it. It is not going to sit around in a jar and go bad. It is going to always be enough for the moment, to fill the glass of Life, to get you through times of disappointment or sorrow, pain or trouble. Knowing God is **with** you fills your cup with joy even in the middle of hard times. All you have to do is turn to Jesus and ask for help.

> This miraculous sign at Cana in Galilee was the first time Jesus revealed His glory. And His disciples believed in Him. After the wedding, He went to Capernaum for a few days with His mother, His brothers and His disciples.
>
> **John 2:11-12**

Another purpose for this miracle was to reveal Himself as God to His disciples. There were six of them at this time – and remember, they had not been with Him for very long. Now that He was on His journey to the cross, God was losing no time in bringing the disciples fully on board, and letting them see His glory. And they believed in Him.

We see His glory today, His Wine of Joy shows up all the time in the lives of people. Jesus is all about changing lives, changing hearts, bringing the joy of His presence into disappointing and difficult circumstances. We see the glory of His Wine at work in our hearts as every time we dip into it we taste forgiveness for our sins and acceptance by God, freedom from shame, and the anticipated joy of a party that will not end. Ever.

Day 9: His Passion

John 2:13-22

Glimpsing the Passion of Jesus

It was nearly time for the Jewish Passover celebration, so Jesus went to Jerusalem. In the Temple area, He saw merchants selling cattle, sheep and doves for sacrifices; He also saw dealers at tables exchanging foreign money.

Jesus made a whip from some ropes, and chased them all out of the Temple. He drove out the sheep and cattle, scattered the money-changers' coins over the floor and turned over their tables. Then, going over to the people who sold doves, He told them, "Get these things out of here. Stop turning My Father's House into a marketplace!"

John 2:13-16

Have you ever seen something that really ticked you off? And it wasn't about you – it was about someone else being hurt or treated unjustly. I remember sitting in the back of a pickup truck with a bunch of high school students, crossing the Mexican-American border into the U.S. to take a break from a mission in Tijuana. We were waiting in line at the border, and saw a bunch of teenage boys begin to beat one boy until they had knocked him on the ground, and then begin kicking him while he was on the ground. As he finally lay motionless, they were still kicking him as we drove through the crossing. Thirty yards from the border, guards everywhere – and no one cared, no one stepped in. Not their problem.

I remember feeling sick to my stomach and frozen, like watching an episode of *CSI,* and desperately wishing someone would do something. I remember envisioning myself jumping out of the truck and running, throwing myself into the fight, rescuing the outcast lying helpless to defend himself. But I did not move.

But in this story, Jesus did. He was angry and acted for all the right reasons. The Temple had a Court for the Gentiles who were searching for the truth, to hear about the One True God from the Jews. This Court had been turned into a market where foreign currency was changed for local currency to service the Jews who came from other regions to worship; then they would buy sacrifices to make to the One True God. So the very market that enabled the Jews to make profit changing money and selling sacrifices for the One True God was actually keeping Gentiles from ever hearing about Him. Conflict of interest, you think?

Jesus acted out the desire to make things right in His Holy Father's place of worship. He acted out of compassion for those who were there seeking the One True God. And He acted to once again reveal that He was God in the flesh as He fulfilled the prophecy in Psalm 69:9: ***"Passion for Your House has consumed Me, and the insults of those who insult You have fallen on Me."***

What are you passionate about? What do you believe in? What would you stand up for and risk being insulted for? Passion is good, it is right, it is glorifying to God when it is passion for the right things. When we think about it, in this story Jesus was being passionate about you. You are the Gentile who was at the temple that day, seeking the One True God, but blocked because you might be kept from Jesus by the greed of men. Jesus was angry ... and He cleared the Temple for you that day. What would you do for Him?

> Then His disciples remembered this prophecy from the Scriptures: "Passion for God's House will consume Me."
>
> But the Jewish leaders demanded, "What are You doing? If God gave You authority to do this, show us a miraculous sign to prove it."
>
> "All right," Jesus replied. "Destroy this Temple, and in three days I will raise it up."
>
> "What!" they exclaimed. "It has taken 46 years to build this Temple, and You can rebuild it in three days?" But when Jesus said "this temple," He meant His own body. After He was raised from the dead, His disciples remembered He had

said this, and they believed both the Scriptures and what Jesus had said.

John 2:17-22

Foreshadowing – it is in every great story, the subtle reference of what is to come. The Jewish leaders were, of course, enraged that Jesus would interrupt their lucrative business. They had rules, they had man-made laws in place, and they demanded Jesus authenticate His authority to make changes. They demanded a miracle. Jesus told them of the miracle of greatest significance for all time. Of course, they missed His foreshadowing, but His disciples remembered later, and like in every good story, they went back and recounted this part again.

The Temple Jesus was talking about destroying was His own body. He was telling them they would crucify Him, destroy Him, but He would rise from the grave in three days. He would become the focus of worship – not this building made of stone and wood. This system of rules of bondage would come to an end, and a new system would be put in place, one of grace and truth.

Grace: receiving what we do not deserve, forgiveness for our sin and acceptance by the God Who made us. Jesus' blood would make us acceptable to God. Nothing else would do. Only His sacrifice.

Creation called back to Creator. Relationship with our Heavenly Father through Jesus Christ.

Now that's something worth fighting for. "Thank You, Jesus!"

Day 10: Being "Born Again"

John 2:23 to 3:8

"ALL IN"

I am not a very good poker player. In fact, I have only played a few times. Some friends of mine invited me to play in a tournament, so I agreed to go, thinking I would just donate the $25 buy-in.

After surviving poker playing for three hours, I went ALL IN on a pair of seven's, which narrowed the game down to just me and my friend Cecil. Eventually, I got tired of playing, and lost on purpose just so it could all be over. I finished in second-place, taking home my winnings of $120. You see, I "believed" I "might" be able to win with a pair of seven's but it was not until I went ALL IN that I actually won the prize.

There is a big difference between believing and committing. People saw the miracles Jesus did and began to believe He was special, perhaps He was more than a great Teacher. But human nature is so fickle; like the prophet Jeremiah said: *"The human heart is the most deceitful of all things, and desperately wicked. Who really knows how bad it is?"* (**Jeremiah 17:9**). Many people believed Jesus **might** be Someone special, but most were not willing to commit, to go ALL IN.

> Because of the miraculous signs Jesus did in Jerusalem at the Passover celebration, many began to trust in Him. But Jesus didn't trust them because He knew Human Nature. No one needed to tell Him what Mankind is really like.
>
> **John 2:23-25**

These very people who would cheer Him for His miracles would one day turn on Him and nail Him to a tree. They believed, but they did not commit. They loved the miracles, but not the Miracle-Maker. They were not ALL IN, but only IN for what was IN IT for them. Jesus still wants commitment today. He was ALL IN for us – He wants us ALL IN for Him. It starts with asking the right questions, like Nicodemus did:

> There was a man named Nicodemus, a Jewish religious leader who was a Pharisee. After dark one evening, he came to speak with Jesus. "Rabbi," he said, "we all know that God has sent You to teach us. Your miraculous signs are evidence that God is with You."
>
> Jesus replied, "I tell you the truth: unless you are born again, you cannot see the Kingdom of God."
>
> "What do You mean?" exclaimed Nicodemus. "How can an old man go

> back into his mother's womb and be born again?"
>
> **John 3:3-4**

Nick was one of the most highly educated Jewish leaders, but had focused his whole life and education on the Law instead of on relationships, on "doing" instead of "knowing." So Jesus told him of a New Law He was bringing: to know God and be known by God through being "born again."

This word "again" is also translated "from above," so Jesus is saying to be part of the Kingdom, to be ALL IN, you must be "born from above."

Nick tries to play stupid here – or really didn't get it – and does his little schtick about how can you enter back into your mother's womb. Preposterous!

> Jesus replied, "I assure you, no one can enter the Kingdom of God without being born of water and the Spirit. Humans can reproduce only human life, but the Holy Spirit gives birth to spiritual life. So don't be surprised when I say, 'You must be born again.'"
>
> **John 3:5-7**

This was news for Nick who – being born a Jew and having kept the Law – assumed he was "in." He was one of God's covenant people. He was exemplary. He had played by the rules.

Surely he was at least better than a Samaritan, or a Gentile, or a Pagan. But now Jesus is telling him there is more than being good, then being righteous. Something has been done for you that you could not do for yourself. Something you need.

Jesus patiently explains to Nick the obvious. First: you must be physically born, which is what "born of water" means. But there is another birth: prompted by the Spirit, when He convicts you of your sin and need for a Savior, and activated by your faith, your decision to believe in a process you can't see or understand. Being born again. This *"birth from above"* is made possible by the decision God made to be the blood sacrifice for our sin. To pay the ransom that was due for our sin. To wash away our sin by the blood and water that flowed out of His side on the cross.

What is our part in this? Believe ... Receive ... Repent ... and Commit. (Repent means to change the way you live, and live to please only Christ. That's ALL IN.)

> The wind blows wherever it wants. Just as you can hear the wind but can't tell where it comes from or where it is going, so you can't explain how people are born of the Spirit.
>
> **John 3:8**

There is so much more here; whole books have been written on just the word "repent." But even Jesus says that you can't really explain what happens inside a person when they are "born again." And that is what faith is all about.

> *Faith is the substance of things hoped for, the evidence of things not seen.*
>
> **Hebrews 11:1**

Your faith activates your birth. Believe ... Receive ... Repent ... Commit. ALL IN!

Day 11: Waters of Birth

John 3:9

Nicodemus Asks What Everyone is Thinking

What happens when a baby is born? While in the womb, we are formed. In the darkness, we hear the sounds of the world beyond but we can't see. We grow, we develop, we become. There is comfort around us. There is water around us and in us, sustaining us, serving us.

The day finally comes: we pass through a birth canal. The waters that once sustained us would now drown us so as we pass through the canal, the waters are squeezed from our lungs ... and we gasp for our first breath of air, our first breath of Life. There are bright lights, there is intensity, it is crazy, loud. We are no longer muffled by waters, and we reach new sensations: cold, hot, smell, touch. We are fully alive with feeling.

John 3 continues with Jesus explaining what it means to be "born again."

> "How are these things possible?" Nicodemus asked.
>
> **John 3:9**

This world is a womb and a birth canal. We are formed through good times and hard times.

We are sustained for a time in this world, we get what we need to exist. We depend on those things always being available to us. Then we hit the birth canal, and the world begins to squeeze us. It is dark, we do not see clearly, sounds are muffled. The things we used to depend on for existence begin to get squeezed out of us. We get tried, tested and our faith is formed. Then – at the very moment we think we may get squeezed to death – as our heads contort and our bodies are wrenched – we emerge. We gasp for air. We let the waters go. We cough, we sputter, we are not quite sure what to do next, but we do what comes naturally. We breathe. We worship. We come to life.

Born from above.

Day 12: The Bronze Snake

John 3:9-17

Jesus Explains Being Born Again

One time I killed a rattlesnake. My wife and I were camping at 25-Mile Creek on Lake Chelan in eastern Washington state. One morning I walked out on the dock of the lake and came upon a rattler. There were children and people everywhere ... so I grabbed my camp shovel and hit it on the head. Kurt 1 / Snake 0.

> "How are these things possible?" Nicodemus asked.
>
> Jesus replied, "You are a respected Jewish teacher, and yet you don't understand these things? I assure you, we tell you what we know and have seen, and yet you won't believe our testimony. But if you don't believe Me when I tell you about earthly things, how can you possibly believe if I tell you about heavenly things? No one has ever gone to Heaven and returned.
>
> "But the Son of Man has come down from Heaven. And as Moses lifted up the bronze snake on a pole in the wilderness, so the Son of Man must be

lifted up so that everyone who believes in Him will have eternal life."

John 3:9-17

Nicodemus was a respected Jewish leader who he came to see Jesus at night. Why? Because he did not want anyone else to know he was checking into Jesus. You see, the Pharisees looked to Moses as their spiritual leader; he was their supreme authority under God. So they hated giving authority to anyone else, including Jesus. It messed with their convenient life of being in control over people.

It is very convenient to follow someone who is dead (Moses) because they can no longer speak into your life, other than what they have already said. But here was Someone new: Jesus, claiming authority to speak into their lives, and saying things that were not in their "Book of Rules." It rocked their world. So Nick at Nite did not want to be seen talking to Jesus because his Law-bound friends might think he is waffling in his commitment to their system and weakening the gang.

So what does Jesus do? He again appeals to Nick's vast knowledge of the Scriptures and reminds him that Moses had predicted His coming. This story Jesus referred to happened in the Book of Numbers 21.

The Israelites had been rebelling and sinning against God, so God sent snakes into the camp to punish them. The people cried to Moses to intercede to God for them, so Moses, their leader, asked God to take away the snakes. Moses was a picture of how Jesus would also intercede to the Father for the sins of the people, and a picture of how God would give grace even though the people deserved death. God responded by giving the Israelites a prophetic picture of Jesus coming to overcome Satan and heal His people of sin.

Instead of taking away the snakes (sin), God told Moses to make a bronze snake and put it up on a pole. Anyone bitten by a snake who looked up at the bronze snake would not die and would be healed. They would still feel the bite of sin, but they would live. This is a story of faith. There was nothing they could do for themselves to rid themselves of the snakes (sin), and once bitten by it, they were destined to die. The only thing that could save them was by faith believing that the solution God offered would save them, and by faith looking up and accepting the grace to be healed. This was a picture of what Jesus would do for all people of all time.

The verb Jesus used, “lifted up,” in the Greek has dual meaning. It means both “crucified” and “glorified.” Jesus was telling Nick that His very crucifixion would also be His means of glory; His crucifixion would be how He was identified as God become human. His crucifixion would carry out the greatest plan of all time: God healing His Creation from the bite of sin and restoring His Creation to Himself. Jesus ends His conversation with Nick by saying these words which are still memorized and spoken today by millions of His followers. He told Nick:

> For God loved the world so much that He gave His one and only Son, so that everyone who believes in Him will not perish but have Eternal Life. God sent His Son into the world not to judge the world, but to save the world through Him.
>
> **John 3:16-17**

How are you "born again"? What is the cure for the snakebite of sin that is killing us all? Lift your eyes to Jesus on the cross, believe by faith that His death and resurrection are the cure for your sin, and your healing will begin.

What about Nick? This conversation burned in his soul for three years. When you are a true seeker, Jesus' words do burn in your soul. You cannot forget what He says. Three years later, when Jesus was finally "lifted up" on the cross, Nick was there. He lifted up his eyes to Jesus and made the connection between Jesus and Moses. He then identified with Jesus by helping take His body down from the cross. He brought 75 pounds (a fortune) of expensive perfume to anoint Jesus' body with, and helped lay Him in the tomb. Nick, a follower of Moses, became a friend of Jesus.

Day 13: Eternal Life

John 3:16-21

Jesus Explains Judgment

God loves us so much that He shrink-wrapped Himself in a human container, and then sacrificed Himself on the Altar of Love for you and for me. The fact is: He could have come to **judge**. He had every right to judge His creation because they had rejected Him.

Eternal Life in Heaven with Jesus is explained in John 3:16-21.

> For God loved the world so much that He gave His one and only Son, so that everyone who believes in Him will not perish but have eternal life. God sent His Son into the world not to judge the world, but to save the world through Him.
>
> **John 3:16-17**

Every person deserves judgment and death because every person has sinned. A holy God cannot co-exist with sin. To forgive sin, there must be sacrifice. Jesus paid the penalty for our sin with His own blood. That is how God pardons each condemned person who will say "Yes" to Him and receive His pardon.

> There is no judgment against anyone who believes in Him. But anyone who does not believe in Him has already been judged for not believing in God's one and only Son.
>
> **John 3:18**

Someone has said, "How could a loving God damn someone to Eternal Death in Hell?" He has **not** – we damn ourselves. We are judged by our own sins and sinful natures. We are judged by our unbelief in a loving God.

God is love, and He offers the same love, acceptance and forgiveness to every person. We decide to accept or we reject it.

All of Creation screams out that there is a Creator, a Designer. Are you ignorant? How can you study Biology, Chemistry, Anatomy, and Physics, but not believe in the Creator? How can you study Botany and Natural Science, but not believe in His Divine Design? The idea that all life – with its mind-blowing diversity and unique DNA – can be traced back to the same pond scum is preposterous. Ignorant.

People who choose to believe in Evolution simply do not want a God to answer to. They do not want to give up control of their life, so they deny God's love. They stay in the dark. No one has an excuse to deny God's love. It is your own rebellion and sinful desire to control your own destiny that resists God's mercy. This will be your judgment, self-imposed, self-sustained.

> And the judgment is based on this fact: God's Light came into the world, but people loved the darkness more than the light for their actions were evil. All who do evil hate the light and refuse to go near it for fear their sins will be exposed. But those who do what is right come to the Light so others can see that they are doing what God wants.
>
> **John 3:19-20**

Each person has the option to eradicate judgment from their life. Each person holds a debit card of grace; it just needs to be activated. One call is all it takes to activate the card and accept God's grace. All we have to do is step into the Light.

Let the Light expose our evil motives, and agree with God that we need His provision to eradicate judgment from our lives. It is a wonderful and awesome thing to be in the Light. In the Light, people see us for who we are. There is no hiding because we are all exposed the same way in the same Light.

Oh, you may pretend you have nothing wrong in your life ... but everyone does. It is a wonderful thing to admit you need grace, and that's what Light does for you. No more hiding. No more lying. No more posing, pretending or faking.

Simply being honest about who you are and what you need. Just like me. Simply living in the Light, and in grace, the undeserved favor of God.
No more judgment. That's freedom.

Whoever the Son sets free is free, indeed!
John 8:36

Day 14: Embracing Change

John 3:21-30

Becoming Less So Jesus Can Be More

Embracing change and moving forward into new things can be painful. Even while I write this, yesterday my family and I moved out of a house where we had lived for the last five years, and we just spent the first night in our new home. This is my reality. Our children are growing and in transition; we are downsizing our lives.

In preparation to build a smaller house, we sold our original house and rented a smaller condo. It has been difficult selling our original house with so many great memories, so much comfort wrapped up in that old home. I liked our home – our life, having lots of room, and a bedroom for each of us. That has all changed ... and after my first night in a new place, I find myself disappointed, anxious and asking questions: *"Was this the right thing to do? Should we have waited another year? Is this too hard on my family? Are they going to be okay through this?"*

Faith is like that. We make our decisions based on what we think God is asking us to do. Still, we do it ... and life changes. And change can be painful.

John 3:22-31 is about Jesus and change.

> Then Jesus and His disciples left Jerusalem and went into the Judaean countryside. Jesus spent some time with them there, baptizing people. At this time, John the Baptist was baptizing at Aenon, near Salim, because there was plenty of water there and people kept coming to him for baptism. (This was before John was thrown into prison.) A debate broke out between John's disciples and a certain Jew over ceremonial cleansing. So John's disciples came to him and said, "Rabbi, the Man you met on the other side of the Jordan River, the One you identified as the Messiah, is also baptizing people. And everybody is going to Him instead of coming to us."
>
> **John 3:22-26**

John the Baptist's disciples were facing huge changes. There was a new Prophet in town, the One their leader had identified as the Messiah. Questions were being raised about the way the Jewish people had done things for hundreds of years. The rules were changing, their world was being shaken. They were asking hard questions. The things they had taken for granted were no longer sure. Jesus had entered the picture, and what they known, believed and counted on their entire life was being challenged. Their comfortable world was disrupted. They went to their leader looking for answers. Looking for comfort.

> John replied, "No one can receive anything unless God gives it from Heaven. You yourselves know how plainly I I told you, 'I am not the Messiah. I am only here to prepare the way for Him.' It is the bride-groom who marries the bride, and the best man is simply glad to stand with him and hear his vows. Therefore I am filled with joy at His success. He must become greater and greater, and I must become less and less."
>
> **John 3:27-30**

The answer John gave them was: *"Move over and let Jesus shine."* He reminds them that it is not about him or them – it is about Jesus. Jesus is the Groom, we (the Church) are the Bride, and John the Baptist is simply the Best Man at the Wedding. His role is to support the Groom and make sure He shines, make sure He succeeds.

It has not become any easier. Change is as hard today as it was back then. I want Life to be about me. The thing that has not changed is the answer to the question: the answer is still Jesus. Letting Him become greater in our lives. When that means moving over and letting go. When that means disrupting our comfort. Struggle. Heartache. Questions. Change.

Day 15: God's "Facebook"

John 3:31-36

John Talks About the Face of God

Do you like *Facebook?* I love it. I get to stay in touch with my friends all over the world. Every day I can hear from my daughter in Scotland, or my son in San Clemente. It is so much fun to share what is happening in our lives.

This morning on my *Facebook* home page, I found photos from friends who are on a mission trip to the Philippines. These friends are still over there, yet I already have their photos. I am seeing and hearing what they are seeing and hearing. Unbelievable!

> "He has come from Above and is greater than anyone else. We are of the Earth and we speak of earthly things, but He has come from Heaven and is greater than anyone else. He testifies about what He has seen and heard, but how few believe what He tells them!"
>
> **John 3:31-32**

Jesus is "the *Facebook* of God." He was in Heaven with God the Father, planning salvation with the Spirit of God, and creating the universe as the Son, the Face of God. The Jews had no problem accepting that Jesus was a great Teacher, even a Prophet. They were okay with the fact that

God may speak to and through Jesus. But to say that He had come **from** Heaven was revolutionary, preposterous, amazing! That would be to say He was God. And that was exactly what John was saying. Jesus is not just passing along some info He picked up along the way. Jesus was there, existed there, knows God because He is One with God, and has come to be God's Face to Humanity. He has come to tell what what He has seen and heard. He is God's *Facebook*.

> "Anyone who accepts His testimony can affirm that God is true. For He is sent by God. He speaks God's words, for God gives Him the Spirit without limit. The Father loves His Son and has put everything into His hands. And anyone who believes in God's Son has Eternal Life. Anyone who doesn't obey the Son will never experience Eternal Life but remains under God's angry judgment.
>
> **John 3:33-36**

I trust Jesus. I believe what He says in His Profile. I believe what He posts on his Home Page. I love the fact that He posts something new and fresh every day. Because we accept what He has seen and heard, we know that God is true. Why? Because Jesus is God's *Facebook.* He told us what He has seen and heard. He is God.

We love the words, *"For God so loved the world that He gave His only begotten Son."* It is important to remember that before God loved the world, He loved Jesus. They are One. Better than the best marriage you could ever imagine. Better than the closest friend you have ever had. God the Father and Jesus are One. Totally unified in thought and action, acting in accordance with one another. Jesus the Son has full authority as God. He wills and acts what the Father wills and acts. Included in this authority is the power to save.

Creation has gone sideways, as Jesus knew it would. Perfect Creation (Humanity) chose to turn from their loving Creator and fully embraced sin. Sin must be judged. There is no other way. It is written in the deep magic of Eternity Past. Sin requires judgment, that is its design. The penalty of this judgment is Eternal Separation from God: Hell. The penalty for sin.

Jesus provided **the Way** to **not pay** ourselves for our sin. He paid it in blood, in sacrifice. The Face of God, defaced for Man. God's *Facebook*. God's message to you.

This life as we know it is our opportunity to see and hear the Son, and through His witness, to be brought back into relationship with God. Believing in Jesus, God's *Facebook*, gives you eternal life.

> *He who has the Son has life; he who does not have the Son, does not have life.*
>
> **1 John 5:12**

Day 16: The Divine Schedule

John 4:1-10

Jesus Breaks the Rules

Ever have one of those days where you feel you are in the right place at the right time? You get to rescue someone ... or you call someone at just the right moment because they needed your call? Jesus had a lot of those days.

In John 4:1-10, Jesus meets a sinful woman.

Jesus knew the Pharisees had heard that He was baptizing and making more disciples than John (though Jesus Himself didn't baptize them - His disciples did). So He left Judaea and returned to Galilee. He had to go through Samaria on the way.

Eventually He came to the Samaritan village of Sychar, near the field that Jacob gave to his son Joseph. Jacob's Well was there, and Jesus, tired from the long walk, sat wearily beside the well about noontime.

Soon a Samaritan woman came to draw water, and Jesus said to her, "Please give Me a drink." He was alone at the time because His disciples had gone into the village to buy some food.

John 4:1-8

The Pharisees were beginning to be a threat, but it was not Jesus' time to end His ministry and die. Notice that everything Jesus does is on Divine Schedule.

There were several routes to Galilee; normally Jews would avoid Samaria because they despised the Samaritans. They were prejudiced against the Samaritans because they were mixed blood: part-Jew and part-Gentile. The Samaritans had even established their own Temple and religious services.

Jesus went this way because His Father had a Divine Appointment for Him. He was tired, weary, and sat down by a well to rest. God in a bod. God shrink-wrapped in a human container – weary like us. Do we get weary sometimes? Tired of Life and its struggles? Jesus understands – He was weary too.

Along comes a woman, and Jesus engages her in conversation. God is not bound by Rules ... He is motivated by Love. The Rules said Jesus was not supposed to even acknowledge this woman. First, because she was a woman, and the Rules said good Jewish men did not talk to single women alone. Secondly, she was a big sinner; she was having sex with someone she was not married to, and she had been married a bunch of times. Third, she was a Samaritan, and the Rules said Jews do not talk to Samaritans. They were considered dirty and unworthy of relationship.

Do you ever feel like you are unworthy of a relationship? Ever feel like maybe God would not want to talk to you? Ever feel like you have done too much wrong for God to want you around or to use you? This woman felt all of those things, and Jesus took the long way to Galilee just to meet her, reveal Himself to her and call her Home. We are never so bad that God does not still care. He hates the sins we commit, but He loves each of us deeply.

Jesus begins the conversation by asking her to do something for Him.

> The woman was surprised, for Jews refuse to have anything to do with Samaritans. She said to Jesus, "You are a Jew and I am a Samaritan woman. Why are You asking me for a drink?"
>
> Jesus replied, "If you only knew the Gift God has for you and Who you are speaking to, you would ask Me and I would give you Living Water."
>
> **John 4:9-10**

The woman was shocked Jesus would want anything to do with her, especially use a cup that had been used by a Samaritan. A Jew would never ask a Samaritan for a favor. Then Jesus did what He does so well: He turned the conversation to her life. He spoke to her situation, and He began by revealing to her Who He was. *"I am God, I have something good to give you, and all you need to do is ask."*

Jesus still says that to us today. *"I am God, I have something good to give you, and all you need to do is ask."* He has Living Water for us. No matter what we face, no matter how we feel, no matter what we have done – Jesus has Living Water for us! He will wash us clean from sin with His Water ... He will save us with His Water ... He will bring us into relationship with God with His Water .. and He will refresh us daily with Living Water. All we need to do is ask. If we only knew what God has for us!

Day 17: Living Water

John 4:10-15

About Being Thirsty

Have you ever been so thirsty you did not care what you drank? I was leading a mission team to Mexico, and after working two or three days in the hot sun, everything looked drinkable. Even the tanked-in water that the locals drank – although we knew we should not drink it – looked appealing.

In Haiti, after about two days, we forgot everything we had been told about the ice cubes. They looked so good and refreshing – how could they possibly make us sick? Boy, did we find out the hard way!

John 4:10-15 is about being thirsty.

> Jesus replied, "If you only knew the Gift God has for you and Who you are speaking to, you would ask Me and I would give you Living Water."
>
> "But, sir, You don't have a rope or a bucket," she said, "and this Well is very deep. Where would You get this Living Water? And besides, do You think You're greater than our ancestor Jacob, who gave us this Well? How can You offer better water than he and his sons and his animals enjoyed?"

John 4:10-12

Good water is like gold, especially in a place where it is hard to find. This woman lived in such a place. Her people had been getting good water from Jacob's Well as long as anyone could remember. Interesting that Jacob's name would come up again. These people revered Jacob, and they revered his water. And Jesus begins to make his comparison of Jacob's water – which is anything this world has to offer – and his Living Water – which is the Life of the Spirit and Eternal things.

> Jesus replied, "Anyone who drinks this water will soon become thirsty again. But those who drink the Water I give will never be thirsty again. It becomes a fresh, bubbling spring within them, giving them Eternal Life."

John 4:13-14

What satisfies you? What makes you feel good? What brings excitement, a sense of fulfillment? What fills you? Is it good food? Is it fine wine? Is it loyal friends? Is it adventure, going to a place you have never been? Is it making love to the one you love? Is it sports? Is it the latest *James Bond* movie? Or perhaps you are one of the millions who has settled into the easy routine of "reality TV" to meet your need for adventure. Being filled by someone else doing an activity that has been scripted, rehearsed and recorded for your viewing pleasure.

All these things have a common factor: they do not last. We thirst again. After the best meal, in a few hours you will be hungry again. After a night out with friends, or after your children leave for college, you will feel alone again. Even the feelings of making love with the one you love do not last. As good as it is, soon you need to feel loved again.

After traveling to some exotic place and posting your pictures on *Facebook,* the memories will fade, and you will desire to experience another place. The smells, sights and senses drift away from our memory like the tiny particles of skin that detach and leave our body when we shower. Useful and even wonderful for a moment, then gone forever down a drain. There is nothing wrong with these things – they are meant to be enjoyed. But they are ... temporary.

This was the Samaritan woman's life: the life of having to go to a water-well every day of her existence. Always thirsty. A life of unhappy marriages, ruin and wreckage. Waking up in the morning, knowing the most significant thing she would do that day was ... go for water.

> "Please, sir" the woman said, "give me this Water! Then I'll never be thirsty again, and I won't have to come here to get water."
>
> **John 4:15**

Oh, to not be thirsty! Oh, to not have to draw water. Oh, to be perpetually content, happy, filled. This world's water has a way of leaving us disappointed so that – like the woman – we long for something better. Something truly good: significance.

We are here on this planet to discover – like the Samaritan woman – the great disparity between what the world has to offer and what God has to offer. It is the ultimate contrast: a great desert where thirst is interrupted by moments of drink – and Life of the Spirit, where we look to Jesus for joy, and long for the ultimate River of Life in Heaven.

A fresh, bubbling spring for day to day living now, giving way to Eternal Life where we will be always filled by the contentment and joy of the Love of God. Feeling entirely enveloped in acceptance, value, significance and love. The longing, the thirst, gone forever. *"Please, sir, give me this Water!"*

Day 18: Clogged Pipes

John 4:15-18

Removing Blockages

The old house I grew up in had steel water pipes. Over the 51 years my parents lived there, the water pressure slowed down until water just trickled out, perhaps one-third of what it should be. When my parents sold their house, the buyers did a complete home makeover, including installing new plumbing. They took out the old steel pipes, filled with the iron rust and gunk built up over the years, and put in brand new plastic pipes. And the water flowed strong at full capacity through the walls of that old house again.

> "Please, sir" the woman said, "give me this Water! Then I'll never be thirsty again, and I won't have to come here to get water."
>
> "Go and get your husband," Jesus told her.
>
> "I don't have a husband," the woman replied.
>
> Jesus said, "You're right! You don't have **a** husband for you have had five husbands, and you aren't even married to the man you're living with now. You certainly spoke the truth!"

John 4:15-18

Sin stops the flow of Living Water in our lives. The woman wanted the Water Jesus had, she wanted to not thirst again ... but He knew she needed to deal with the blockage of sin in her life. She needed new pipes, she needed to confess her sin, she needed forgiveness. Jesus knew she had been married five times, and still He told her to get her husband. He graciously gave her an opportunity to confess her sin – that she was not married to the man she was living with – then He led her to agree with Him about her sin.

The first step to letting the Living Water flow in our lives is identifying there is a blockage. We do that by being aware of what Jesus wants of us by reading His Word, and identifying the things in our lives that do not agree with His Word. Then we confess those things to Him, agree with God that those are sins, and get them out of our lives. That is what we must do to have a good flow of Living Water. Living Water cannot flow where there are bad attitudes, bitterness, unforgiveness, harshness with the ones we love, angry words, unconfessed sin. So we must work with Jesus to keep the pipes clear.

Of course, the first step is to get new pipes. *"Out with the old, in with the new."* We get new pipes when we turn your houses over to the new Owner, Jesus. Get a complete home makeover. Agree with Jesus that we want and need Living Water. Agree with Him we need new pipes by identifying the old pipes are filled with rust and sludge, gunk from the past, and ask Him to forgive us. Get rid of the gunk-filled pipes through the power of the Cross, complete forgiveness for our sins.

So now we have new pipes. How do we keep our new pipes from filling with gunk again? We confess the gunk every time it happens, and let the Living Water wash it away. Sin likes to cling on to the wall of a pipe, much like cholesterol to an arterial wall. Keep the flow strong by confessing sin and asking for forgiveness. Turn away from old patterns of living and maintain our new pipes through reading God's Word, spending time talking with Jesus, and dedicating our new Living Water System to letting everyone we meet know just how good this Water is!

Day 19: A Revolutionary Statement

John 4:19-26

A Most Unlikely Confidante

Ever been in a conversation where you feel so uncomfortable that you change the subject? Someone asks you a question that threatens to expose you, so instead you quickly bring up a new topic.

That is what this Samaritan woman was doing. Just a second before, Jesus had exposed her sin and convicted her for living with a guy to whom she was not married. She knew she was dealing with Someone Who knew a lot more about her than she was comfortable with. She acknowledged He was a prophet – in other words, He had the power to know what He had no way of actually knowing – and so she changed the subject.

> "Sir," the woman said, "You must be a Prophet. So tell me, why is that you Jews insist that Jerusalem is the only place of worship, while we Samaritans claim it is here at Mount Gerizim, where our ancestors worshipped?"
>
> **John 4:19-20**

She asked the question: *"Where should we worship?"* Today the question might have been: *"Where should we go to church? Which one is right, is best?"* Jesus wanted to discuss her heart – and she changed the subject to religion. Jesus wanted to be real with her – and she deflected Him. Jesus wanted to lovingly expose sin and provide a solution – and she avoided Him like the plague. Sounds familiar?

Okay, okay, let's explain the worship question. The Jews worshiped in the Temple in Jerusalem, and they had a certain way to worship, with lots of rules and regulations, mostly man-made and man-imposed, not God's idea. They had a system, it was working for them, and they didn't want anyone messing with it.

About the Samaritans, Warren Wiersbe tells us:

> *The Samaritans were a mixed race, part-Jew and part-Gentile, that grew out of the Assyrian captivity of the ten northern tribes in 727 BC. Rejected by the Jews because they could not prove their genealogy, the Samaritans established their own Temple and religious services on Mount Gerizim. This only fanned the fires of prejudice. So intense was their dislike of the Samaritans that some of the Pharisees prayed that no Samaritan would be raised in the resurrection!*
>
> ~ **Warren Wiersbe**

In short, the Jews had a corner on worship, and hated the Samaritans even more for having their own twist on it. All the more reason that Jesus should not have been talking to this woman!

> Jesus replied, "Believe Me, dear woman, the time is coming when it will no longer matter whether you worship the Father on this mountain or in Jerusalem. You Samaritans know very little about the One you worship, while we Jews know all about Him, for salvation comes through the Jews. But the time is coming - indeed, it's here now - when true worshippers will worship the Father in spirit and in truth. The Father is looking for those who will worship Him that way. For God is Spirit, so those who worship Him must worship in spirit and in truth."
>
> **John 4:21-24**

Everyone thinks their way of worship is the right and best way. The Jews had the most knowledge of understanding about and history with God. God revealed Himself through the Jews, and entrusted them with the revelation of Him to their world. But they had complicated worship ... and as we found out in John 2 on Day 9, Jesus was angry about that. So He cleared the Temple.

Now Jesus makes a revolutionary statement that has to do with His coming and with His leaving. His coming would do away with the middle man. No longer would they need priests to make sacrifices for them to absolve their sin. Jesus' sacrifice would take care of all sin for all time.

No longer would they need a Temple made of wood and stone to worship in. The place of worship would be each heart of each person who received His sacrifice. He would make the way clear for every person to go directly to God instead of through men and ritual. His leaving would usher in the presence of the Holy Spirit, available for the first time to all people. In the past, the Holy Spirit had come to a select few – like prophets, priests, kings, His mother Mary, His aunt Elizabeth, and some others. Now all people would enjoy the presence of God living in them. They would now worship God under the direction and presence of the Holy Spirit in them, in the Truth of the Son of God that would unite creation with their Creator.

> The woman said, "I know the Messiah is coming - the One Who is called Christ. When He comes, He will explain everything to us."
>
> Then Jesus told her, "I Am the Messiah!"
>
> **John 4:25-26**

Again, understand how preposterous it is that Jesus – a Jewish teacher and a man – would share something of this magnitude with a woman

... and a Samaritan at that! Jewish rabbis had a saying: *"It is better that the words of the Law be burned than be delivered to a woman!"* (cited by Warren Wiersbe).

I do not want you to miss how important it is: Jesus **did not care** what people thought of Him. God made a point of shattering people's ideas of what was "right." He cared for, accepted and invested in the lowest of the low. Perhaps this is the most important message hidden in this discussion of worship. Perhaps true worship is really how we treat each person made in the Image of God. (Hmm, I think Jesus says something like that later on.)

Jesus then does the unthinkable: He utters the words that would put Him on a cross. He shared His secret with a broken, ruined and wrecked woman, who lived a life filled with the pain of her wrong choices – but also a woman desperate for the Living Water. It is the thirsty ones who most desperately need a drink. And Jesus gave her the drink when He revealed Himself to her.

"I AM the Messiah." Jesus uttered the words that Jews feared to utter, the name of God: *"I AM."* He said, *"I AM God in the flesh. I AM God revealed to you today. I AM the Living Water. I AM."* He still IS!

Day 20: Jesus' Big Secret

John 4:26-30

A Lesson in Sociology

Then Jesus told her, "I AM the Messiah!"

John 4:26

Let that sink in to your soul. Meditate on that for a while. What does that mean to you?

Just then, His disciples came back. They were shocked to find Him talking to a woman but none of them had the nerve to ask, "What do You want with her?" or "Why are You talking to her?"

John 4:27

The disciples were scandalized. It was their first big lesson in sociology from Jesus. Out with the morés and social norms – in with the love of God. Out with prejudice and archaic ideas – in with the acceptance of God. Notice, however, that Jesus did not go soft on sin. He still called a spade a spade. Living with someone before marriage was still fornication, and He called out the woman on it ... but He did it with grace and truth, not judgment. He risked the trust of His disciples because He cared for this Samaritan. She was not just some woman – she was one of His own lost sheep.

The woman left her water jar beside the well and ran back to the village, telling

> everyone, "Come and see a Man Who told me everything I ever did! Could He possibly be the Messiah?" So the people came streaming from the village to see Him.
>
> **John 4:28-30**

There was an American TV show called *Lost.* Were you a fan of *Lost*? What if you were lost with some people on a desert island. You had already drank all the water you had with you, and now you are desperate for more. People are dehydrated, some are sick and no longer active. As you comb the island, looking for water, you come across a clear, bubbling spring. Water, and plenty for all.

Would you tell them? Or would you hoard it for yourself and let them die? There is plenty for all. How fast would you run to the other people? Someone could die in the moments you linger. They need water to live, and they need it now.

Do you have the Living Water? Will you share it? It is the humane thing to do.

Day 21: Soul Food

John 4:31-38

Food From Another World

Jesus tells us about what keeps Him going in this life, in John 4:31-38.

Ever walk into a conversation and misunderstand what was being said? That is how rumors start. The disciples were constantly misunderstanding Jesus because they were so wrapped up in their physical, practical world ... and Jesus was always thinking about the real world, the Eternal World. The world He had left to come to Earth. They were talking about food that fueled the body – Jesus was talking about food that fueled the soul.

> Meanwhile, the disciples were urging Jesus, "Rabbi, eat something."
>
> But Jesus replied, "I have a kind of food you know nothing about.
>
> "Did someone bring Him food while we were gone?" the disciples asked each other.
>
> **John 4:31-33**

What keeps you going in this world? What makes living worthwhile for you? Is it making money? Having good friends? Doing fun stuff? Getting the right career? What makes you get out of bed in the morning? What do you believe in and throw yourself into?

> Then Jesus explained, "My nourishment comes from doing the will of God Who sent me, and from finishing His work. You know the saying, 'Four months between planting and harvest'? But I say: 'Wake up and look around! The fields are ripe for harvest.'
>
> "The harvesters are paid good wages, and the fruit they harvest is people brought to Eternal Life. What joy awaits both the planter and the harvester alike! You know the saying: 'One plants and another harvests'? And it's true. I sent you to harvest where you didn't plant; others had already done the work, and now you will get to gather the harvest."
>
> **John 4:34-38**

I started picking strawberries when I was seven years old. All day we would work in the hot fields, and as the day dragged on, my hands moved slower and slower. It seemed like everyone else advanced down the row except me. The berries – which should have been my motivation – became my enemy because I just could not pick them fast enough. After three or four hours, my one crate of berries – which should have been full in thirty minutes – had reduced itself to strawberry jam in the hot sun.

One day I had a fantastic idea. Here I was, sitting in a row of dirt, with clods all around me. Why not pick up clods and add them to my harvest? *(Sorry, Mr. Clark, if you're just now finding out about this.)* If I put clods on the bottom of the boxes under the berries, no one would know. Clods were heavier and so my crate would weigh more, and I would get paid more ... or so reasoned my 7-year-old mind. Who would know?

It only worked once. The next day, the now-stern-faced field boss gathered us together and assured us if any one was caught putting dirt under their berries, they would be fired and lose all their income from the season. *(I guess Mr. Clark found out after all!)*

The fact is: strawberries were the harvest ... and I was picking dirt. Much of what we do in Life is picking dirt. It may work for a while, it may even get our ticket punched for a time. We may even find a sense of fulfillment as we fill the bottom of our boxes. But at the end of the day, you do not get paid for picking dirt.

The disciples came back from town with food, and Jesus taught them a lesson: There is something even more important than the food we eat. More important than a roof over our heads. More important than going to school, getting a degree, having a 6-figure income, seeing the world. True significance and true nourishment of the soul comes from picking the right fruit. And what is the right fruit? Anything you say or do that influences a person's Eternity. Any act of service you do to advance the Kingdom of God.

Maybe it is helping teach kids in the church Children's Ministry, or being a leader for Youth Group. Maybe it is coming alongside someone who needs spiritual guidance. Maybe it is inviting someone to church, or hosting a Small Group, or leading a Small Group. Maybe it is making a meal for someone.

I can see Jesus, pointing to the woman and the villagers as they came back toward them, saying to the disciples: *"Here is what fuels Me. This is what ignites My soul. Here comes the harvest now, walking toward us. In fact, one of them has already been harvested: this woman."*

We are here to pick strawberries: the hearts and eternal future of real people. All we have to do is keep our hands moving and advance down our row. God will fill our boxes with Eternal Fruit. This is where true significance comes from in this life. This is how our souls are fed.

Do you feel empty? Useless? Depressed? Give yourself to something greater: the Harvest. Get in the right field. Start picking the right fruit. There is nothing more thrilling than influencing someone for Christ. Not only do you feel the joy of it on this Earth, but you will be paid great wages when you turn in your punch card to Jesus.

Day 22: Hanging Out With Outcasts

John 4:39-42

Jesus "Reads Our Mail"

I feel like an outcast sometimes. Most people don't like to hang out with pastors. They think we are not normal Maybe they feel like I will be judging every word they say, scrutinizing every action. But the truth is, pastors are real people too. They have feelings, think bad thoughts, commit real sins, and need to be watered and fed like everyone else. Jesus was great with hanging out with those who were cast out. He still hangs out with them.

> Many Samaritans from the village believed in Jesus because the woman had said, "He told me everything I ever did!" When they came out to see Him, they begged Him to stay in their village. So He stayed for two days, long enough for many more to hear His message and believe. Then they said to the woman, "Now we believe, not just because of what you told us but because we have heard Him ourselves. Now we know that He is indeed the Savior of the world."
>
> **John 4:39-42**

It is one thing to hear about someone, it is another thing to get to know Him for yourself. The Samaritan woman convinced many of her neighbors that Jesus was the Messiah because He had "read her mail." He had told her things about her life that He could not possibly know in the natural. She was convinced in her heart that He was the Messiah, and her conviction influenced the people in her life.

There is another layer to believing, however. It is the believing that comes when you move from "knowing about" to "knowing." It is moving from "having information about" to "having experienced intimate connection with." These villagers begged Him to stay because they wanted to get to know Him.

Clearly, Jesus wanted to get to know them too. He stayed two days with the people who were outcast from His society. He broke a lot of Jewish rules to be with them. His disciples were probably worried about what people would think if word got back that they had stayed in an unclean village with unclean, outcast Samaritans. But Jesus stayed. And they believed. He was God in the flesh.

No matter what our spiritual conditions, no matter what our living conditions, Jesus will stay if we want to get to know Him. He will be with us in the worst of situations. His condition: He wants us to want to know Him.

When we spend time with Jesus, we end up knowing Him. We end up believing Him because we hear from Him ourselves, not just about Him.

He will stay with us in our village, in our house, in our room, if we ask Him. Even if we feel like outcasts. He is just waiting to be invited.

John writes another book called "Revelation." At the end of his life, he wrote it based upon visions he had while in exile on an island. In one of the visions he saw his beloved Savior and Friend Jesus once more. Here is what John heard Jesus say:

> "Look! I stand at the door and knock. If you hear My voice and open the door, I will come in, and we will share a meal together as friends."
>
> **Revelation 3:20**

Day 23: Four Kinds of Faith

John 4:43-53

What Brings Us Closer to God?

Ever had a crisis in your life? Ever prayed, *"God, if You will just get me through this test with an A, I promise I will study next time"* or *"God, if You help me get a date with Joe, I promise to stop hitting my sister"*? As much as we do not like crises, it is most often difficulty and struggle that brings us to God.

> At the end of the two days, Jesus went on to Galilee. He Himself had said that a prophet is not honored in His own hometown yet the Galileans welcomed Him, for they had been in Jerusalem at the Passover celebration and had seen everything He did there.
>
> As He traveled through Galilee, He came to Cana, where He had turned the water into wine. There was a government official in nearby Capernaum whose son was very sick. When He heard that Jesus had come from Judaea to Galilee, he went and begged Jesus to come to Capernaum to heal his son who was about to die. Jesus asked, "Will you never believe in Me unless you see miraculous signs and wonders?"
>
> The official pleaded, "Lord, please come now before my little boy dies."

> Then Jesus told him, "Go back home. Your son will live!" And the man believed what Jesus said, and started home. While the man was on his way home, some of his servants met him with the news that his son was alive and well.
>
> He asked them when the boy had begun to get better, and they replied, "Yesterday afternoon at one o'clock, his fever suddenly disappeared!" Then the father realized that this was the very time when Jesus had told him, "Your son will live." And he and his entire household believed in Jesus. This was the second miraculous sign Jesus did in Galilee after come from Judaea.
>
> **John 4:43-54**

Crises bring us to God. When things are going well, we just don't think about Him as much. We cruise in our own strength, we enjoy the comfort of the moment. Oh, we do not lose focus intentionally – we just are not intentional about our focus. Crises keep us sharp, seeking, dependent, desirous, desperate.

That is where this government official was: he was desperate for God. His son was dying. There was no where else to turn. Who knows if he would ever have turned to Jesus were it not for this crisis?

No one likes crises, of course; I do not like crises any more than you do. I am not suggesting you go out looking for them so that you will be more aware of your need for God. That being said, crises in our life give God an opportunity shine, to be present, to be our strength. They give us an opportunity to build our faith by turning to God and trusting Him. It is called Crisis Faith. Faith for the moment. Faith of desperation.

Problem is: that is where our faith stays. We only look for God in the crises of life. God wants our **Crisis Faith** to mature into **Confident Faith.** Confident enough to "go back home." Jesus told the official to *"go back home"* – in other words, *"Do not let the Crisis consume you. Go about your daily business and have faith that I am working."*

I will bet the official was thinking about taking Jesus hostage and making Him go with him until his son was healed. But the official *"went back home"* – his Crisis Faith became Confident Faith, confident that God was Who He said He was. Confident that He would be true to His Word. God wants our Crisis Faith to become Confident Faith, so that when there is a crisis, our faith is already confident that God will see us through.

We shall not stop there. God wants our Confident Faith to become **Confirmed Faith.** Confirmed Faith means that when God does work in our crisis, we give Him credit, and it makes believers out of us. The boy was healed.

Now the official could have said – like we do sometimes – *"What a coincidence! What a coincidence that the fever left my son at the same time as Jesus told me he was healed."* But no, the official allowed his Confident Faith to become Confirmed Faith. He believed. Confirmed Faith means we live in the awareness that God is **always** at work in our situations, in our lives. We look for Him. **We expect Him.** We try to discern what He is doing so that we can partner with Him in the crises of others. We ask the question, *"God, what is Your will through this situation?"*

When Crisis Faith gives way to Confident Faith, and Confident Faith gives way to Confirmed Faith, we become people of **Contagious Faith.** Our faith influences others. We talk about it. We share it. We show it. We live it.

That official went home, his entire household noticed the change in him; they believed his testimony about what had happened, and they believed in Jesus too. He became contagious. When you become contagious, people get infected. Contagious Faith infects others. You can't help yourself. You are Contagious.

(Thanks to Warren Wiersbe, for use of the "four faiths.")

Day 24: Chronic Conditions

John 5:1-7

Everyone Wants to Be Well

"Would you like to get well?" Jesus asks.

> Afterward, Jesus returned to Jerusalem for one of the Jewish holy days. Inside the city, near the Sheep Gate, was the Pool of Bethesda, with five covered porches. Crowds of sick people - blind, lame or paralyzed - lay on the porches. One of the men lying there had been sick for 38 years. When Jesus saw him and knew he had been ill for a long time, He asked him, "Would you like to get well?"
>
> "I can't, sir," the sick man said, "for I have no one to put me into the pool when the water bubbles up. Someone else always gets there ahead of me."
>
> **John 5:1-7**

The Pool of Bethesda was said to have healing powers. When the water began to bubble, people who were able to arrive in the water first were said to be healed. This sick man had been trying to get in the water for years. Jesus asked him a strange question: *"Would you like to get well?"* What kind of a question is that? Of course, he would want to get well, wouldn't he?

But the man's answer is just as strange: *"I can't,"* he said. Why did he not just say yes?

"Yes, I want to get well! Yes, of course I do!" Instead, he made excuses about why he had not yet been healed.

Have you ever made excuses about the way you are? Justified your condition? Blame others for *"getting there ahead of you"*? Sometimes it seems easier to just stay the way we are than to say, *"Yes, I want to get well"* – and then do the work of getting well. Especially with chronic conditions of the soul.

Some people who have a chronic condition of the soul just lay by the pool instead of making the changes they need to embrace healing and change. Chronic conditions of the soul include: the *"Poor Me"* syndrome ... the *"Bitter for What Has Happened to Me"* syndrome ... the *"Never Get Any Breaks"* syndrome ... and the *"I Am Not Very Gifted"* syndrome, to name just a few. People who give in to these syndromes tend to lay by the pool and feel sorry for themselves. They do not break out of their chronic condition of the soul because they do not believe they can. So they stay stuck. And they develop habits that keep them stuck.

Jesus comes along and asks, *"Do you want to get well?"* – but instead of just saying "Yes," they justify why they are still laying by the pool. Then Jesus says, *"Stand up, pick up your mat, and walk."*

Jesus told him, "Stand up, pick up your mat, and walk!" Instantly the man was healed! He rolled up his sleeping mat and began walking.

But this miracle happened on the Sabbath, so the Jewish leaders objected. They said to the man who was cured, "You can't work on the Sabbath! The Law doesn't allow you to carry that sleeping mat."

But he replied, "The Man Who healed me told me, 'Pick up your mat and walk.'"

"Who said such a thing as that?" they demanded. The man didn't know, for Jesus had disappeared into the crowd.

But afterward, Jesus found him in the Temple and told him, "Now you are well, so stop sinning, or something even worse may happen to you." Then the man went and told the Jewish leaders that it was Jesus Who had healed him.

John 5:8-15

Sometimes others don't like it when we get healed. Healing brings change. We become stronger persons, more confident, able to care for ourselves. Some people need us to stay sick because they want us dependent on them.

Some people don't like the process we might go through to change. It may involve counseling, which can be messy for awhile. We may feel things we are not comfortable feeling. We may have some hard questions for the ones we love. That's okay – we will get through it with Jesus' help.

Change may involve breaking the power of secrecy over family secrets. Change may include grieving what we have never been allowed to grieve: the loss of innocence, incidents of abuse. When we are healed, we are able to walk on our own. We don't need people to carry us everywhere we go. Some people feel more comfortable carrying us than letting us walk.

The Jews had rules against carrying burdens on the Sabbath. That is why they were angry at this man: because he was carrying his bed on the Sabbath. They were more concerned about a stupid rule than the fact that he had been healed by Jesus.

People still have rules today. Families have rules, and sometimes the rules are not healthy, not there for your benefit. They are there to keep the family "looking good." Healing and change sometimes means challenging the status quo, challenging the "normal," the "way it has always been."

Remember: if you want to get healed, and you want to stay healed, then stop sinning. Do not sin against others as you pursue healing. If you have been sinning – perhaps even to cope with your chronic condition of the soul – Jesus says stop. Good things happen to those who say “Yes” to Jesus.

Day 25: Jesus Is God

John 5:16-18

Going Public

People love control. They love power. They love to rule with fear over people. The Jewish religious leaders had built a system that worked for them because it kept them in control of the people, and it gave them power. They had rules in place, man-made rules that kept the people under their thumbs. Jesus began to challenge these rules because He was God, and He knew which rules He had given, and which ones He had not.

Like doing good on the Sabbath, or healing someone on the Sabbath, or setting a man free from demons on the Sabbath. These were all things which glorified God but "broke the rules." By challenging the system, Jesus was revealing Himself as God. He was beginning to unwrap the Big Commandment: *"Love God, and Love Your Neighbor."* The Jews did not like it. They could feel their domination over the people slipping away from their grasp.

> The Jewish leaders began harassing Jesus for breaking the Sabbath rules. But Jesus replied, "My Father is always working, and so am I." So the Jewish leaders tried all the harder to find a way to kill Him, for He not only broke the Sabbath, He called God His Father, thereby making Himself equal with God.
>
> **John 5:16-18**

On this day, Jesus had raised the stakes for the Jews to hate Him and try to kill Him. He called Himself God. He claimed God not only as "our Father" but as "My Father." It was acceptable to refer to God as Father from a collective viewpoint, but not from a personal stance. Jesus made it personal with the statement *"**My** Father."*

In the Jewish culture, the son had all the rights and privileges, honor and authority of the father. On some future day, the Jewish first-born son would inherit all ... and in the present, a Jewish first-born son could be given authority to act in proxy for his father. Sort of like "durable power of attorney." He could conduct business on his father's behalf. Jesus was doing His Father's business.

That is what Jesus was saying to the Jews. By calling God His Father, He made Himself equal to God. They hated that, and hated Jesus for it. From that moment on, they began to plan ways to kill Him.

Jesus is God.

Day 26: The Father and the Son

John 5:19-23

It Is In the Relationship

> So Jesus explained, "I tell you the truth: the Son can do nothing by Himself. He does only what He sees the Father doing. Whatever the Father does, the Son also does."
>
> **John 5:19**

If you want to blame someone for healing on the Sabbath, blame the Father. Wow! Talk about stirring up a bucket of snakes! Jesus was telling the Jewish leaders, *"Look, I cannot do this stuff on My own. Without the Eternal God being in Me, I am just a man like you. But because the Eternal God is in Me, I cooperate with what He wants to do. He wants to heal on the Sabbath – I go along with it. I do what that Father does. You want to blame someone for breaking your rules? Blame God!"*

> "For the Father loves the Son and shows Him everything He is doing. In fact, the Father will show Him how to do even greater works than healing this man. Then you will be truly astonished."
>
> **John 5:20**

I am a father; I have two children. My children have friends they bring home. Some of them become close friends of my children. Because my children love them, I accept them and love them too. But make no mistake: the love I have for my children is greater. My loyalty is to my children. My children are my priority. Why? Because they are a part of me. I am committed to their well-being.

If Lindsey said, *"Dad, we need to let Susie live with us; she needs us"* – I would say, *"Okay."* But the primary reason I would agree is because of my great love for Lindsey. I know her, I am committed to her, and I would do anything for her.

That is a very imperfect picture of how God the Father loves the Son. The Son came from Him, is a part of Him, and They agreed on a plan of salvation for this Creation made in Their image: us. Yes, God the Father loves us, but it is because He loves His Son. You might say God the Father loves us through Jesus. It is important to remember that the Father and the Son are One.

> "For just as the Father gives life to those He raises from the dead, so the Son gives life to anyone He wants. In addition, the Father judges no one. Instead, He has given the Son absolute authority to judge so that everyone will honor the Son, just as they honor the Father. Anyone who does not honor the Son is certainly not honoring the Father Who sent Him."

John 5:21-23

Warren Wiersbe wrote these three ways God the Father is revealed through Jesus Christ the Son:

1. *His **Works** – Jesus revealed the Eternal God through the miracles He performed, the people He healed, and particularly the ones He raised from the dead. The Jews believed there were three keys only God held: (i) to open the heavens and give rain; (ii) to open the womb and give conception; and (iii) to open the grave and raise the dead. For Jesus to do this would be the ultimate revelation to the Jews that He was God.*

2. *His **Judgment** – The Jews believed that only God the Father could judge anyone for their sin and works. Here Jesus re-educates them, letting them know that He, the Son, will have "absolute authority to judge." It makes sense. Jesus is the Creator of all, so why would not He be the Judge of all He created?*

3. *His **Honor** – Jesus makes it clear to the Jews that if they do not honor Him, they are not honoring the Father. Wow! Talk about drawing a line in the sand. Think of how shocking this would be to the Jews. For centuries they had been honoring God with their system of sacrifices. Now they are hearing from this God-Man that the way to honor God the Father is by honoring the Son. By receiving the Son. By recognizing the Son as their ultimate Judge.*

Can you start to see why they wanted to kill Him? He was messing with their system.

The claim is clear, and sets us apart from every other religion: Jesus Christ is the Way to the Eternal God. Those religions which claim to worship God the Father, Jehovah, but do not recognize Jesus as God, are cults. Not because of what I say but because of what Jesus said. The only way to worship the Father is through the Son. That is how God set it up. Know the Son and you know the Father. Receive the Son, and you have Eternal Life with the Eternal God.

Day 27: The Walking Dead

John 5:24-30

We All Experience At Least One Resurrection

Zombie movies have always scared me. The idea that you can kill someone and they keep coming after you, over and over, relentlessly, is horrifying to me. No matter how many times you shoot them, burn them, hack them, they keep coming back. The walking dead.

> "I tell you the truth: those who listen to My message and believe in God Who sent Me, have Eternal Life. They will never be condemned for their sins, but they have already passed from death into life. And I assure you that the time is coming - indeed, it's here now - when the dead will hear My voice, the voice of the Son of God. And those who listen will live."
>
> **John 5:24-25**

Jesus called us "the walking dead." How does it feel to be dead? Did we understand we have already been dead? Jesus said that until we receive Him, we are dead. And when we receive Him, He gives us life and a pass from walking death into Eternal Life. The First Resurrection.

If we have received Christ, we have already experienced one resurrection. Passing from death into life. Jesus said, *"The 'walking dead' (us) will hear My voice – the voice of the Son of God. And those who listen will live."*

What does it mean to be the walking dead? It means its all over for us when this "life" ends. It means that no matter what we do with our lives – no matter what we accomplish, no matter who we impress or what success we have – outside of Christ it is all meaningless and insignificant. Outside of Christ, it is all "dead works" that will perish and be forgotten when we die and pass on.

It is only when we receive Christ's life in us, the resurrection power of the cross, that we "come to life" in our spirits, our inner persons. We aren't alive until we "come to life" by receiving Christ. Once we receive Christ, all that we do for Him and His Kingdom has significance and will be remembered and rewarded. Life.

> "The Father has life in Himself, and He has granted that same life-giving power to His Son. And He has given Him authority to judge everyone because He is the Son of Man."
>
> **John 5:26-27**

The Second Resurrection is the resurrection we most commonly think of, especially at Easter: it is the resurrection of Jesus Christ Himself. The Father holds all life in Himself – He did not need anyone else to resurrect Christ. He gave the resurrection power to Jesus, and Jesus was resurrected and received a new, perfect eternal Body, a prototype of the body we will receive. Along with resurrection power, Jesus also has the authority to give life to anyone who receives Him, and to judge anyone who does not. This Resurrection is the most important of all, because it made all other resurrections possible.

> "Don't be so surprised! Indeed, the time is coming when all the dead in their graves will hear the voice of God's Son, and they will rise again. Those who have done good will rise to experience Eternal Life."
>
> **John 5:28-29a**

The Third Resurrection. We who have been resurrected from the "walking dead," we who have received Christ, will experience this resurrection too. When Jesus Christ comes again in His glory and power, we who have the life of Christ in us will hear and recognize His voice because we are His. We have been purchased by His blood. The life of Christ in us will respond to the voice of our Savior, and we will be physically resurrected. We will be given new, perfect, eternal bodies that will live with God forever. Bodies that can withstand and embrace the glory of the presence of Almighty, Eternal God.

> "And those who have continued in evil will rise to experience judgment. I can do nothing on My own. I judge as God tells Me. Therefore, My judgment is just, because I carry out the will of the One Who sent Me, not My own will.
>
> **John 5:29b-30**

The Fourth Resurrection is "the resurrection of the walking dead." It is also called the "Resurrection of Condemnation." We already mentioned those who have "done good" – we who have received Christ. That is the only truly "good" thing we could do to inherit Eternal Life: just believe. But what about all the other people who lived on this Earth and did not embrace the opportunity to know God through receiving Christ?

Warren Wiersbe says: *"Believers will be given resurrection bodies so that they might reign with Christ in glory. Unbelievers will be given resurrection bodies – but not glorified bodies – that they might be judged and then suffer punishment in those bodies. Bodies that were used for sin will suffer the consequences of that sin."* The walking dead will suffer their own consequences of not embracing the Eternal Life which God provided.

What mystifies me is why anyone would say "No" to Jesus. If we have walked this Earth for very long, we already know it is filled with disappointment and insignificance, momentary pleasures that fade away like the last light of day in the evening sky. Knowing Jesus gives us hope, joy, purpose, and significance.

Jesus has provided Life and the Way to know God. Living for Him on this Earth is the only way to really enjoy significance and a sense of purpose, especially as we help other dead people "come to Life." He wants us to each enjoy a vibrant, living relationship with Him on this Earth, and Life with Him in Heaven forever.

Embrace Jesus. Come to Life.

Day 28: Easy and Difficult

John 5:31-46

Pondering Belief

What does it take for us to believe something? Do we have to see it with our own eyes? Do we have to hear it from a reputable source? Do we have to touch, taste or smell it? How do we believe in a God we may not encounter with our five senses? Faith.

> "If I were to testify on My own behalf, My testimony would not be valid. But someone else is also testifying about Me, and I assure you that everything he says about Me is true. In fact, you sent investigators to listen to John the Baptist, and his testimony about Me was true.
>
> "Of course, I have no need of human witnesses, but I say these things so you might be saved. John was like a burning and shining lamp, and you were excited for a while about his message. But I have a greater witness than John: My teachings and My miracles. The Father gave Me these works to accomplish, and they prove that He sent Me. And the Father Who sent Me has testified about Me Himself.
>
> "You have never heard His voice or seen Him face to face, and you do not have

His message in your hearts because you do not believe Me - the One He sent to you. You search the Scriptures because you think they give you Eternal Life. But the Scriptures point to Me! Yet you refuse to come to Me to receive this Life."

John 5:31-40

What does it take to believe? Jesus gave the Jews lots of reasons to believe.

First proof: there was John the Baptist. John was recognized as a significant prophet, the son of a priest, a miracle-baby, born to a barren woman who was too old to have children. John's whole life was lived in preparation to validate Jesus Christ as the Son of God.

Second proof: Jesus gave them miracles and teaching – things they had never seen or heard before. And there would be many more miracles to follow. One miracle might have been enough, but He performed miracle after miracle ... and still they did not believe. His teaching was like no other, revolutionary and visionary, bringing to life the words that had settled into tradition.

What does it take to believe? They had the witness of a prophet, the proof of miracles, but they also had the thing they valued above all else: the third proof – the Holy Scriptures. They loved the Holy Scriptures; they worshiped the words of Moses and the Prophets of old. They studied and studied, believing they would discover secrets of the Coming Messiah in between the pages.

The Holy Scriptures – the very words they valued above all else – confirmed Jesus as Messiah. Jesus was the fulfillment of prophecy, things that had been foretold hundreds of years before. And they would not see it. He did not fit their idea of who God should be, what a messiah should look like or accomplish. They wanted someone who would liberate them from the Romans, not someone who would set captives free from sin and the grip of Satan. From His conception to His ascension, Jesus would fulfill **108 prophecies** foretold about the One Who would come to save. But they would not see it. They would not believe it. They would not let their vast knowledge generate faith in their hearts to believe. They let their heads get in the way.

What does it take to believe? Just **faith**. Aren't you are glad God chose faith to be our response to His invitation for Eternal Life. I mean, He could have chosen a high IQ, which would have disqualified billions of people ... He could have established a minimum level of affluence in order to make it in to Heaven ... He could have even made good deeds the measure of getting to Heaven. Too bad for the thief on the cross, who used his faith in his dying moments to believe in Jesus, dying next to Him.

God said, *"Just believe."* The easiest and most difficult thing to do. Easy, because anyone can do it – difficult, because it requires giving in to the mystery and majesty of God. Easy, because it makes sense of the condition of our world – difficult, because there is so much we still do not know. Easy, because we desperately want someone to love and accept us for who we are – difficult, because sometimes it is hard to believe anyone could.

Faith. We cannot see it, but it has substance. It has power. It is more real than the chair I am sitting on, because what it believes in is eternal.

- Faith: it is the substance of things hoped for.
- Faith: it is the evidence of things you cannot see.
- Faith. Do not let your head get in the way.

Day 29: *"Jesus, I Believe"*

John 5:41-47

About Approval

Whose approval do you long for? Who is it you try to please? To what lengths do you go to impress certain people? Is it your friends? Your spouse? Your parents? People who don't know you well? The general public? That cute guy, or the beautiful girl?

Take a moment and think about what you do daily and why you do it. Does the need for approval drive your life? Think about how you relate to people. Does the need for approval keep you from being honest, from speaking the truth in love to those you meet? Why do you care what people think about you? Why does it matter what they think?

Jesus was effective in carrying out His Father's will because He did not let what people thought of Him change the way He lived out His Father's will.

> "Your approval means nothing to Me because I know you don't have God's love within you. For I have come to you in My Father's Name, and you have rejected Me. Yet if others come in their own name, you gladly welcome them. No wonder you can't believe! For you gladly honor each other, but you don't care about the honor that comes from

the One Who alone is God."

John 5:41-44

There is only one Person Who loves us completely and purely, without ulterior motivation, without a hidden agenda. He is the One Who made us and knows us; we bear His image. He is the only One Whose approval matters. Why? Because He is the only One Who truly accepts us for who we are, and loves us in spite of our failures. He holds our Eternity in His hand.

Why do we work so hard to gain the approval of people? Because we want to be accepted. We long for connection. We were created for connection. We deeply believe in our souls that somehow we can earn and keep that connection with people. We deeply believe we need that approval and connection to live.

News Flash: we do not need the approval of people to live. If we think we do, we live our lives dishonestly, not open before people, always hiding, faking, acting. Hoping for a good review for our performance. We do not need it.

That being said, then why care about what people think? Because we care for them. **It is not about getting approval – it is about giving compassion.** People need love because people need Jesus. We have Jesus, so we love people.

It is about Jesus. Jesus did not show compassion to people to earn their approval – He showed compassion because He knew they needed Him. If we are going to be like Jesus, we must accept and care for people because they need God, not because we need their approval. People are precious. God loves each person, no matter how we feel about them.

The reason Jesus was angry with the Jews is because they knew the Scripture, inside and out. They had it memorized and could quote it. They put all their hope in knowing and following the Law of Moses. They knew the letter of the Law, but they missed the heart of the Law: LOVE. They worked so hard to look good in each other's eyes, to stay on top of their game, to earn approval ... but they forgot about loving. They were so obsessed with looking good they forgot about **being** good. Jesus would sum up the Law later when He gave them a new commandment: *"To love God with all their heart, soul, mind and strength; and to love their neighbor as their own self"* (Mark 12:30-31).

As we walk with Jesus, we care less and less about getting the approval of people. The approval of people is a fickle thing ... and most often, as we try to get it, we compromise our ability to live honestly. We try to be what we are not to get what we do not need. Life is about loving people, serving people, and enjoying the approval of our loving Heavenly Father.

Love God. Be yourself. Love people. God approves.

Day 30: Story Problems

John 6:1-15

Pop Quiz On Faith

After this, Jesus crossed over to the far side of the Sea of Galilee, also known as the Sea of Tiberias. A huge crowd kept following Him wherever He went because they saw His miraculous signs as He healed the sick. Then Jesus climbed a hill and sat down with His disciples around Him. (It was nearly time for the Jewish Passover celebration.) Jesus soon saw a huge crowd of people coming to look for Him. Turning to Philip, He asked, “Where can we buy bread to feed all these people?” He was testing Philip, for He already knew what He was going to do.

Philip replied, “Even if we worked for months, we wouldn’t have enough money to feed them!”

Then Andrew, Simon Peter’s brother, spoke up, “There’s a young boy here with five barley loaves and two fish. But what good is that with this huge crowd?”

“Tell everyone to sit down,” Jesus said. So they all sat down on the grassy slopes. (The men alone numbered about 5,000.) Then Jesus took the loaves, gave thanks to God, and distributed them to the people. Afterward He did the same with the fish. And they all ate as much as they wanted.

After everyone was full, Jesus told His disciples, "Now gather the leftovers, so that nothing is wasted." So they picked up the pieces, and filled twelve baskets with scraps left by the people who had eaten from the five barley loaves.

When the people saw Him do this miraculous sign, they exclaimed, "Surely He is the Prophet we have been expecting!" When Jesus saw they they were ready to force Him to be their king, He slipped away into the hills by Himself.

John 6:1-15

In Algebra class in school, I hated story problems. They gave you the beginnings of a great story, like: "*Michael is in a dark forest in Eastern Europe, running away from an assassin. He has to run 300 yards in 45 seconds to reach safety. His assailant has to run 400 yards to catch him. If Michael has run 250 yards in 30 seconds and his assailant has run 300 yards, how many seconds will it take the assailant to catch Michael if ...?*"

What I hated about story problems – other than I could never find the answer – was that you never found out the end of the story. It was frustrating!

Maybe that is why I majored in Psychology instead of Math.

Here we have a great story and we have a math problem: *"There are 5,000 hungry men plus wives and kids. A little boy has 5 loaves of bread and 2 fish. How much faith will it take for Jesus to multiply the lunch to feed the crowd and end up with 12 baskets full?"* The answer? It did not take much faith, and Jesus still did the miracle because He cared about the people. Now that is a great story problem!

What I love about this story problem is that, first of all, it is not a problem for God. Secondly, we get to find out the end of the story. Here is the first lesson of the day: **God is not bothered or hindered by an impossible economy.** He still takes what we bring Him, and makes the most of it to meet the needs of the moment. That is a good thing to remember today as the World Economy is facing gargantuan problems.

The other thing that grabs my attention about this story is verse 6, which says: *"He (Jesus) was testing Philip, for He already knew what He was going to do."* Do we think about the fact that Jesus tests those He loves? The fact that He tests us proves He loves us? Why? He wants us to grow in our faith. He wants us to remember what we have learned. He knows its good for us to learn that He is faithful.

The disciples should have remembered a similar incident when a certain wedding party ran out of wine. Jesus took water and made it into the best *Shiraz* (at least, that is what I think). If we could take water and make wine, do we think we could take rocks and make loaves of bread? So Jesus was testing His disciples, and He picked Philip first.

And here is the interesting thing: He already knew how Philip was going to respond. Would it have been fun for Philip to pass the test? Of course! Instead of giving the negative answer, *"We would not have enough,"* what if instead Philip had said, *"Jesus, I believe You can!"*

What are your tests today? Nearly every day brings a test. What have you learned from walking with Jesus? Has He been faithful? Has He come through in the past? Has He met you where you are at and gotten you through difficulties and disappointments? Then He can do it again.

Philip was predictable, and Jesus knew what he would say. How about we surprise Jesus and give the right answer: *"Jesus, I believe you can do it,"* whatever IT is!

Today when we are tested (and we will be), would it be fun to pass the test? No more of the *"I do not have enough grace / strength / compassion / forgiveness in my heart / peace / joy / love"*-type answers Instead, try answering: *"Here is what I have, Jesus. Please take it, break it, multiply it, bless it. I believe You can make it enough for this situation, right here, right now."*

Jesus, I believe.

Day 31: Becoming

John 6:16-21

Strengthening Character

There is a storm coming. As I write this, I can hear the wind increasing outside. All the local meteorologists have been making the most of it, saying its going to be a bad one. I love storms – as long as I am safe and warm inside, and the people I love are safe and warm. Storms remind me of how good it feels to be secure. Storms give me a good excuse to hunker down, turn on the fireplace and enjoy a great book. But sometimes storms come into our lives and it's not much fun at all. Like this one:

> That evening, Jesus' disciples went down to the shore to wait for Him. But as darkness fell and Jesus still hadn't come back, they got into the boat and headed across the lake toward Capernaum. Soon a gale swept down upon them and the sea grew very rough.
>
> They had rowed three or four miles when suddenly they saw Jesus walking on the water toward the boat. They were terrified, but He called out to them, "Don't be afraid. I am here!" Then they were eager to let Him in the boat, and immediately they arrived at their destination!
>
> **John 6:16-21**

There are all kinds of storms in our lives, and they come for many different reasons. Some storms are just the storms of Life, like the economic storm we are in right now. They come, and – because we live in this fallen world – we have to go through them with everyone else.

There are the storms that come as a result of bad decisions we make. These are the storms of our consequences. Jonah had a storm of consequence. The best thing to do when these storms come is to take responsibility, repent, make the changes necessary to be insure this storm doesn't happen again, and make it up to the people who got dragged through the storm with us. **Learn from these storms.** Learn wisdom and obedience.

Then there are the storms like the story we just read. These are the storms God puts in our lives to test us and grow our faith. Did you think Jesus did not know about this storm? He knew, all right. He knew there was a storm coming ... and in Matthew's account of this story, he tells us that Jesus insisted they get in the boat and cross to the other side of the lake. The disciples found themselves in this storm **because** they obeyed Jesus. ***"What?!?*** *I thought if I obey Jesus, Life will be smooth and easy."* Sorry, that is bad theology.

Following Jesus in obedience may just put us in the middle of a big storm. John the Baptist was obedient to Jesus ... and lost his head. All the disciples were obedient to Jesus ... and eventually lost their lives, painfully. Christians today in India and around the world are experiencing big storms and even losing their lives because of obedience to Christ.

"Why then," you ask, *"would I be obedient to Christ?"* Because being a follower of Christ is not about Life being smooth and easy. It is not about comfort in this Life. It is not about skating through unscathed. It is about **becoming**.

Becoming less dependent on self and more dependent on Jesus. Becoming less self-centered and more Jesus-centered. Becoming less a Person of Fear and more a Person of Faith. In Matthew's account, after rescuing His disciples, Jesus said to them, *"You have so little faith; why did you doubt Me?"*

When storms comes into our lives, and we have been doing our best to be obedient to Jesus, it is great to ask the question: ***"What?"*** Usually, we ask the question: *"Why?"* – as in, *"Why are You allowing this storm? Why did You let this happen to me?"*

Maybe a great question to ask would be: *"**What**? What are You doing with me? What do You want me to learn? What are character strengths are You growing in me? What needs to change in me? What am I ... **becoming**?"*

Becoming. Sometimes that is what the storm is about. Becoming.

Day 32: Only Believe

John 6:22-29

Simple Faith

What does God want from us? The answer is found in John 6:22-29.

Here we see the crowds the day after Jesus fed them. Through the night, His disciples learned a valuable lesson about Jesus and storms. So now, about breakfast time, when the people begin to get hungry, they begin to think about Jesus. They begin to think about food. Funny how we begin to think about God when we get hungry, thirsty, lonely, desperate.

> The next day, the crowd that had stayed on the far shore saw that the disciples had taken the only boat, and they realized Jesus had not gone with them. Several boats from Tiberias landed near the place where the Lord had blessed the bread and the people had eaten. So when the crowd saw that neither Jesus nor His disciples were there, they got into the boats and went across to Capernaum to look for Him.
>
> They found Him on the other side of the lake, and asked, "Rabbi, when did You get here?"
>
> Jesus replied, "I tell you the truth: you want to be with Me because I fed you,

not because you understood the miraculous signs. But don't be so concerned about perishable things like food. Spend your energy seeking the Eternal Life that the Son of Man can give you. For God the Father has given Me the seal of His approval.

John 6:22-27

Jesus redirects their focus. They come to Him for physical food, and He tells them to use more energy seeking spiritual food. Then He sets them up for a great conversation. You see, Jesus wants them to know that the Bread-Giver also is the Life-Giver. We go to Him for many needs, and our focus is usually the practical, but He re-directs us too. He reminds us that at the end of the day what we really need is Eternal Life, not just bread.

They replied, "We want to perform God's works too. What should we do?"

Jesus told them, "This is the only work God wants from you: believe in the One He has sent."

John 6:28-29

People tend to try to gain God's approval by doing good works, by being good people. For some, that means being a Shriner. For some, it means serving on City Council. For some, it means giving money to a worthy cause. We call these good works. These works are all GOOD

THINGS, but not worth ANYTHING for Eternity unless the main work has been accomplished.

There is only one work we could do that really pleases God: BELIEVE.

- Believe in Jesus Christ.
- Believe He is God.
- Believe He came to seek and save the lost.
- Believe He died on the cross and rose again so we could have your sins forgiven and have Eternal Life.

God revealed Himself to His Creation through Jesus Christ. He wants us to believe.

Believe.

Day 33: *"I AM Bread"*

John 6:29-40

The Staple of Life

What do you eat when you are hungry? Some people like sweets; I tend to look for something salty, like chips or nuts. I love smokehouse almonds, but I would have to say my favorite snack of all time is *Planters Dry Roasted Cashews*. No other brand will do. There is something about the taste of *Planters Dry Roasted* that just does it for me. How about you?

For the people in Jesus' day, it was bread. But bread was not just a snack – bread was essential to live. Bread was considered to be Life, especially for the Jews. Why? Because one of the most famous miracles God had performed for them was to feed them with a type of bread, *manna,* when they were starving in the wilderness. They did not have *Lays* or *Tostitos* or *Pringles.* They had fresh bread.

Why were they seeking Jesus? They wanted more bread! They told him, *"Come on, Moses did it. He did a miracle and gave us bread in the wilderness."* They wanted Jesus to feed them, and He had. They wanted another miracle.

Most people initially seek Jesus because they want something from Him. They need bread, or a miracle of some sort. Jesus often responds by doing something miraculous in the life of one who seeks Him. But then He turns the corner with each of us. Instead of giving us more bread, He says, *"I am the Bread."* Instead of making every circumstance of life work for us, He says, *"I am Life."* He wants us to leave the road of thinking we must have all our wants met in order to be happy, and turn the corner into a life where all our needs are met in Him. He is the Bread. He is Life. We need to believe that HE is all we need.

> Jesus told them, "This is the only work God wants from you: believe in the One He has sent."
>
> They answered, "Show us a miraculous sign if You want us to believe in You. What can You do? After all, our ancestors ate manna while they journeyed through the wilderness! The Scriptures say, 'Moses gave them bread from Heaven to eat.'"
>
> Jesus said, "I tell you the truth: Moses didn't give you bread from Heaven – My Father did. And now He offers you the True Bread from Heaven. The True Bread of God is the One Who comes down from Heaven and gives life to the world."
>
> "Sir," they said, "give us that bread every day."
>
> **John 6:29-34**

There are many Christians around the world today who actually live this out. It is possible to live a life centered on Jesus being your sustenance, not what you get out of Life. Christians in Haiti – who for their one meal per day – eat an avocado. Christians in Orissa, India, who live every day under the pressure of knowing they may be persecuted and even die that very day. Jesus becomes their Bread. Jesus becomes their Life. He becomes their Everything.

It is challenging to look to Jesus to be your Everything when you already have everything. For us in the West, it becomes a choice. We realize the comforts we enjoy do not really feed us or fill us; they certainly do not give us Life. Still, we easily become distracted by them. That is why Jesus said it is easier for poor people to enter His Kingdom: they have less distractions. People of means have a harder time clearly seeing Jesus as Bread and Life. We make our own bread, we buy our own life.

> Jesus replied, "I AM the Bread of Life. Whoever comes to Me will never be hungry again. Whoever believes in Me will never be thirsty. But you haven't believed in Me even though you have seen Me. However, those the Father has given Me will come to Me and I will never reject them.
>
> "For I have come down from Heaven to do the will of God Who sent Me, not to do My own will. And this is the will of God: that I should not lose even one of those

He has given Me, but that I should raise them up at the Last Day. For it is My Father's will that all who see His Son and believe in Him should have Eternal Life. I will raise them up at the last day."

John 6:35-40

Six of the most important verses in all of Scripture. Jesus says, "I AM." This is very significant because in Jewish religion, only Almighty God used the words, "I AM." Jesus lays out the plan of salvation: that they would believe He is God and He has come to save. That anyone who believes in Him, He will raise up to eternal life at the end of all time.

This is Bread. This is Life. Are you hungry?

Day 34: Small, Round and White

John 6:41-51

Continuing Revelation

I love Christmas. I love to give gifts to those I love. The fact I love to give to the ones I love reflects something about my Father in me. You see, He also loves to give gifts to the ones He has created and who bear His image: Us.

> Then the people began to murmur in disagreement because He had said, "I AM the Bread that came down from Heaven." They said, "Isn't this Jesus, the Son of Joseph? We know His father and mother. How can He say, 'I came down from Heaven'?"
>
> But Jesus replied, "Stop complaining about what I said. For no one can come to Me unless the Father Who sent Me draws them to Me, and at the Last Day, I will raise them up. As it is written in the Scriptures: 'They will all be taught by God.' Everyone who listens to the Father and learns from Him comes to Me. (Not that anyone has even seen the Father; only I, Who was sent from God, have seen Him.)"

John 6:41-46

Jesus is a gift to us. Salvation is a gift. We can do nothing to earn it. In fact, if it were not for God drawing us through His Word and His presence, we would not ever have even noticed Him, like so many others in the world. There is nothing we can do to enhance, improve or deserve this gift. He does not prefer one person over the next. He offers everyone the same gift.

What are our choices when someone offers us a gift? Receive the gift, or refuse the gift. Jesus said:

> "I tell you the truth: anyone who believes has Eternal Life. Yes, I AM the Bread of Life! Your ancestors ate manna in the wilderness, but they all died. Anyone who eats the Bread from Heaven, however, will never die. I AM the Living Bread that came down from Heaven. Anyone who eats this Bread will live forever; and this Bread, which I offer so the world may live, is My flesh."
>
> **John 6:47-51**

Warren Wiersbe does a great job of helping us understand how *manna* was a picture of Jesus, the Bread of Life, to the Jews:

> *It is not difficult to see in the* manna *a picture of our Lord Jesus Christ. The* manna *was a mysterious thing to the Jews; in fact, the word* manna *means "What is it" (see Exodus 16:15). Jesus was a*

mystery to those who saw Him. The manna *came at night from Heaven, and Jesus came to this Earth when sinners were in moral and spiritual darkness. The* manna *was small (His humility), round (His eternality) and white (His purity). It was sweet to the taste (see Psalm 34:8) and it met the needs of the people adequately.*

The manna was given to a rebellious people; it was the gracious gift of God. All they had to do was stoop and pick it up. If they failed to pick it up, ***they walked on it.*** *The Lord is not far from any sinner. All the sinner has to do is humble himself and take the Gift that God offers.*

Over and over we see symbolism of Jesus Christ throughout Scripture. The Bible is all about Jesus. The Old Testament prophecy gives us a look at Who He is and predicts how He would come. Jesus fulfilled 108 Old Testament prophecies by His coming. The New Testament tells us all about what He did and how to receive Him.

It is all about Jesus. Receive the Gift.

Day 35: Smells So Good!

John 6:51-59

The Food of Eternity

When I was a boy, I loved Saturday mornings. On Saturday mornings I would go next door to my Aunt Mona's house. Saturday morning was the day she baked fresh crescent rolls.

When you walked through the door into her house, the smell was like everything good that has ever been. She would give me a fresh, hot roll with a huge glob of butter on top, and I would watch cartoons in her living room (*The Fantastic Four, Space Ghost, Superman, Aqua Man, Batman*) while eating it. It does not get much better than that for a 6-year-old boy. To this day whenever I smell fresh bread, I think of my Aunt Mona.

Jesus knew how important bread was to the Jewish people. It was Life to them. They came to Him hungry for bread, and He did a miracle so they could be fed. But more than that – He did the miracle to help them make the connection between Bread and the Bread of Heaven, Life and Eternal Life.

> "I AM the Living Bread that came down from Heaven. Anyone who eats this Bread will live forever; and this Bread, which I will offer so the world may live, is My flesh."

> Then the people began arguing with each other about what He meant. "How can this Man give us His flesh to eat?" they asked.
>
> **John 6:51-52**

Was Jesus telling them they literally had to eat His flesh? Of course not! He was saying that just as we need bread to sustain us day to day, if we take Jesus into our hearts, we will have Eternal Life. If we choose to partake of Him and His sacrifice for us, we will live forever with Him.

> So Jesus said again, "I tell you the truth: unless you eat the flesh of the Son of Man and drink His blood, you cannot have Eternal Life within you. But anyone who eats My flesh and drinks My blood has Eternal Life, and I will raise that person at the Last Day. Anyone who eats My flesh and drinks My blood remains in me and I in him."
>
> **John 6:53-56**

Perspective is so important. Remember, Jesus is coming from Eternity Past, where bread is not a mixture of flour and water. In Eternity, what sustains us is the presence of Eternal God. It is only for a short time on this Earth that we need bread. For Eternity – beginning with the day we receive Christ here on Earth – our souls feed on Him, His Word, His presence. It is Jesus and His sacrifice that we need for Eternal Life, not the bread of flour and water. From an eternal perspective, Life begins with and is sustained by receiving and ingesting the Bread of Life, Jesus Christ.

> "I live because of the living Father Who sent Me; in the same way, anyone who feeds on Me will live because of Me. I am the True Bread that came down from Heaven. Anyone who eats this Bread will not die as your ancestors did (even though they ate the manna) but will live forever." He said these things while He was teaching in the synagogue in Capernaum.
>
> **John 6:57-59**

So, with what do we feed our souls? Do we smell the sweet goodness of Jesus and have a piece of Him daily? Do we feed upon the promises of His Word, to be sustained and filled with encouragement and hope? Do we find ourselves drawn daily by the thought of fresh bread? Do we snack throughout the day on sweet morsels of conversation with Him, sharing our thoughts, and inviting Him into every moment?

Mmmm! Smells so good!

Day 36: *"Where Else Would We Go?"*

John 6:60-70

Jesus Brings A New Way

It was scandalous! After hundreds of years of keeping the Ten Commandments, working hard to keep every bit of man-made Jewish Law, staying clean and making sacrifices to be acceptable to God, Jesus was giving them a new way.

He was the Messiah they had believed in and waited for – but they were having a difficult time giving up old ways. Sound familiar? In fact, they were offended by Jesus telling them all they needed to do to have Eternal Life was to believe and accept Him. In prophecy, Jesus was called the Cornerstone that the people rejected, a Rock that they would stumble over. This was being fulfilled.

> Many of His disciples said, "This is very hard to understand. How can anyone accept it?"
>
> Jesus was aware that His disciples were complaining, so He said to them, "Does this offend you? Then what will you think if you see the Son of Man ascend to Heaven again? The Spirit alone gives Eternal Life. Human effort accomplishes nothing. And the very

words I have spoken to you are spirit and life.

"But some of you do not believe Me." (For Jesus knew from the beginning which one didn't believe, and He knew who would betray Him.) Then He said, "That is why I said that people can't come to Me unless the Father gives them to Me."

John 6:60-65

"Human effort accomplishes nothing." To some, that is a terrifying statement because they have always depended on their abilities to make life work. To others, that statement is the best thing they have ever heard, and they are ready to give up and give in to Jesus, to really receive and enjoy what He accomplished FOR them.

I love the fact that I cannot do anything to earn right standing with God, just believe by faith. And even that faith comes from God, as Jesus reminds us that God draws us to Jesus through truth, His Word. All we can do is give in to it and let God have His way in our life. I love that.

Jesus reminds us that it is not about what we can do – it is about the Word, the truth He speaks. As we receive and ingest His Word, we are taking in spirit and life.

Not everyone can handle this gracious plan. They would rather think they can accomplish right standing with God by their human effort. Like many of the people there that day.

> At this point, many of His disciples turned away and deserted Him. Then Jesus turned to the Twelve and asked, "Are you also going to leave?"
>
> Simon Peter replied, "Lord, to whom would we go? You have the words that give Eternal Life. We believe, and we know You are the Holy One of God."
>
> Then Jesus said, "I chose the twelve of you, but one is a devil." He was speaking of Judas, son of Simon Iscariot, one of the Twelve, who would later betray Him.
>
> **John 6:66-70**

Many times, Peter's words have echoed in my mind:

"Lord, if we left You, to whom would we go?
When I feel alone – where else would I go?
When I'm not feeling close to God – where else would I go?
When I'm disappointed by those I love – where else would I go?
When this world falls apart around me – where else would I go?
When I FEEL like checking out, leaving Jesus, going my own way – where else would I go?"

When we want life, hope, a future, peace in a stormy world, eternal security, it does not make sense to go anywhere else. Jesus has the words that give Eternal Life.

Day 37: Timing

John 7:1-9

Jesus Reveals His Father's Timing

Timing is everything. Especially at the holiday season when we are making things like candy or special sauces, or cooking chocolate. When making holiday candy or sauces, the right ingredient added at the wrong moment can ruin the sauce. A little sugar added 30 seconds too early can ruin the candy. We all love water and need it to live, but get a little water in your chocolate ... and your glossy, shiny, beautiful chocolates become dull and ugly. You know what I mean? Something said a week too early can have a different effect than the same thing said at the perfect moment, the moment God provides.

Jesus was perfectly tuned to His Father's timing. He knew the perfect moment for Him to accomplish the work He was sent for: His sacrificial death and resurrection. He knew if He went to Judaea, the chances were very high he could be arrested, even killed. The time was not right. He was scheduled to die at Passover, to fulfill prophecy about Him.

Human wisdom said: "Now is the moment. Go now, work some miracles, get some attention, and You will build Your Kingdom." His own brothers did not understand who He was and why He had come. But Jesus knew. And His Father knew. God had a perfect moment reserved for Him to be arrested and die.

> After this, Jesus traveled around Galilee. He wanted to stay out of Judaea, where the Jewish leaders were plotting His death. But soon it was time for the Jewish Festival of Shelters, and Jesus' brothers said to Him, "Leave here and go to Judaea, where Your followers can see Your miracles! You can't become famous if You hide like this! If You can do such wonderful things, show Yourself to the world!" For even His brothers didn't believe Him.
>
> **John 7:1-5**

People outside of Christ do not have to worry about God's timing. Oh, He may have a plan for them – like He did for Herod, for Judas, for Pilate – but they do not know about it and they are not concerned about it. Humans are pretty predictable in our sin, and will do what humans normally do: stay committed to self. But Jesus was on an eternal timetable, and so are we. Anyone who has the Holy Spirit in them are on God's timetable; we sometimes just don't ask the question, "Is now the right time?" Jesus was always asking that question.

> Jesus replied, "Now is not the right time for Me to go, but you can go anytime. The world can't hate you but it does hate me because I accuse it of doing evil. You go on. I'm not going to this Festival because My time has not yet come."

After saying these things, Jesus remained in Galilee.

John 7:6-9

Jesus was really saying to His brothers, *"You can go anytime you want because it is inconsequential what you do. It has no bearing on the Kingdom. However, what I do with My minutes and days has great bearing, and brings eternal consequences."* (Kurt's interpretation)

We are on God's *DayTimer.* We are on His planner. If we are His, then He has a plan for us today. It may not involve us getting to the cross at the perfect moment (or it may). I would say most often this plan involves the right word spoken at the right moment.

Words have power. James tells us that words have the power of life and death. What we choose to speak at any given moment brings life or death to someone's life. We might say, "That is too much responsibility for me. I will just say nothing then, I will play it safe." Sorry, it does not work that way. A word left unspoken at the opportune moment may leave life unspoken to someone who needs life.

Words. It may be a tender, loving word to a spouse who needs it today. It may be a loving word of correction to a teenager at the perfect moment. It may be a word of affirmation to a 3-year-old that will set a course in their life to believing about themselves what God believes about them. We may speak a word from God to someone today. In fact, I would expect and hope we would.

What is a word from God? It is a word for the moment, a morsel of truth, a dash of exhortation, a teaspoon of love (thanks, *Mary Poppins*), a savory word for the perfect moment. Something, of course, which lines up with truth from God's Word. Something said that points a person to Christ.

Every believer should be listening to God at every moment for the right word for that moment, spoken for the benefit of that person. Sometimes we wield "truth" as a personal sword; that is not what I am talking about. Rather, we should use truth skillfully as a surgeon would use a sharp blade, for the benefit of another, and at no benefit to ourselves. Other than the satisfaction of knowing we have been used by our Father to help accomplish His work in the life of another of His children.

Look for God's timing today, and ask Him what we could say to add to the moment. If we cannot think of anything, it always feels good to hear the words, "I love you." And remember the wise words of *Thumper's* mother (from Disney's *Bambi*): *"If you REALLY can't say somethin' nice, don't say nothin' at all!"*

Day 38: Knowing the Truth

John 7:10-24

What Lies Beneath

Don't you love a person who goes against the flow, stands up against the crowd? I love people like that, especially when they are gifted, popular or beautiful people. I love people who could do or be whatever they want because of the gifts and abilities they have, yet they choose to take a stand for Truth.

Jesus stood for Truth, He went against the grain. He stood up to the crowd, the religious mafia who tried to keep him down. Jesus would not let them suppress Him; instead, He caused quite a stir wherever He went. People were always trying to figure out Who He was and what He was about. His teachings were controversial but they rang with Truth to those who really had a heart to listen.

> But after His brothers left for the Festival, Jesus also went, though secretly, staying out of public view. The Jewish leaders tried to find Him at the Festival and kept asking if anyone had seen Him.
>
> There was a lot of grumbling about Him among the crowds. Some argued, "He's a good man," but others aid, "He's nothing but a fraud who deceives the people." But no one had the courage to

> speak favorably about Him in public, for they were afraid of getting in trouble with the Jewish leaders.
>
> Then, midway through the Festival, Jesus went to the Temple and began to teach. The people were surprised when they heard Him. "How does He know so much when He hasn't been trained?" they asked.

John 7:10-15

I love this part! Jesus knew so much about the Scriptures **because He was there when it happened.** He was teaching out of experience of being God, not from something He had learned in rabbinical school. That is why His teaching was so compelling – He taught like no other because He had lived it like no other: **He lived it as God.** He could speak the Word because He **is** the Word.

> So Jesus told them, "My message is not My own; it comes from God, Who sent Me. Anyone who wants to do the will of God will know whether My teaching is from God or is merely My own. Those who speak for themselves want glory only for themselves, but a person who seeks to honor the one who sent him speaks truth, not lies."

John 7:16-18

Why do some people accept Jesus, and some do not? Jesus tells us why: people who really want to know God are drawn by His Truth. His Word is Truth. Jesus is His Word. So people who want to do the will of God accept Jesus. People who want to live for themselves do not accept Jesus. It is that simple. Why?

They listen to the same lie Satan told Adam and Eve in the Garden: *"You can be like God. You can run your own life."* People want to run their own lives, live for their own glory. They buy the lie that they are free when they run their own lives. They do not want to give up control of their lives and live in obedience to their Maker.

Those who do bring their lives under God's authority find there is freedom in obedience. Jesus said it like this: *"You will know the truth, and the truth will set you free"* (John 8:32). These very people who claimed to follow truth were law-breakers. They were murderous in their hearts, and Jesus knew it. He knew what was beneath the surface.

> "Moses gave you the Law, but none of you obeys it! In fact, you are trying to kill Me."
>
> The crowd replied, "You're demon-possessed! Who's trying to kill you?"
>
> Jesus replied, "I did one miracle on the Sabbath, and you were amazed. But you work on the Sabbath too when you obey Moses' law of circumcision. (Actually,

> this tradition of circumcision began with the Patriarchs, long before the Law of Moses.) For if the correct time of circumcising your son falls on the Sabbath, you go ahead and do it so as not to break the Law of Moses. So why should you be angry with Me for healing a man on the Sabbath? Look beneath the surface, so you can judge correctly."
>
> **John 7:19-24**

What lies beneath? In the life of every person is a heart that is drawn by Truth. Like a needle on a compass is drawn to True North, our hearts are drawn by Truth. It is the lie of Satan that blocks the Truth, it is deception that confuses the spiritual compass. Speakers of Truth, livers of Truth, help to set the compass straight. We go against the tide, we live for God instead of ourselves. People see. People notice. People are drawn by Truth. Live for the Truth so people can know the Truth and be set free.

Day 39: The Messiah

John 7:25-31

Good News!

What is the biggest news you ever heard? Usually it is bad news. Recently, I stepped out of my front door and looked down my street to see 7 or 8 Sheriff cars and 2 CSI vans parked in front of a house. Deputies were taking measurements and pictures in the front yard.

Apparently at 11:00pm the night before, while I was catching up on the bad news from around the world, bad news was happening just a few hundred yards from my front door. People were shot. A man was killed ... and I had not heard a thing.

> Now some of the people of Jerusalem were saying, "Is not this the Man Whom they are trying to kill? And here He is, speaking openly, but they say nothing to Him! Can it be that the authorities really know that this is the Messiah? Yet we know where the Man is from; but when the Messiah comes, no one will know where He is from."
>
> Then Jesus cried out as He was teaching in the Temple, "You know Me, and you know where I am from. I have not come on My own. But the One Who sent Me is true, and you do not know Him. I know

> Him because I am from Him, and He sent Me."
>
> Then they tried to arrest Him, but no one laid hands on Him because His hour had not yet come. Yet many in the crowd believed in Him and were saying, "When the Messiah comes, will He do more signs than this Man has done?"
>
> **John 7:25-31**

Can you feel the passion erupt from the Son of God as He cries out to His created ones, His own children? Here He is in the Temple, the very place designed for people to worship God, and He is God ... yet they do not recognize Him. He so passionately longs for His people to know Him, to receive Him, to allow Him to gather them unto Himself. His desire for His loved ones pours out of Him, His humanness unable to contain the pure love of God.

This is how He feels about you, about me. He wants us to know Him, be one with Him. So He reveals Himself to us over and over again. Can you hear Him crying out for you?

It was still not God's time for Jesus to taken, because God had planned for Him to die on the Passover ... and remember, He was the Lamb of God.

Day 40: Trouble

John 7:32-36

"Bring It On!"

Trouble. Did we ever think that following Jesus might get us into trouble? It can, depending on the amount of risk we are willing to take for Him.

I have a friend who, back in the 70's, used to smuggle Bibles into Eastern Europe. He risked finding trouble. I have another friend who trains leaders of the Underground Church in China. Lots of trouble to be found. I have other friends who live in India and teach Bible to potential leaders. As you may have heard, Christians are not real popular in India these days. They are being beaten and burned. Trouble.

Following Jesus can get you in trouble here in the States too. Standing up for Jesus can get you into trouble with the School Board, the PTA or the Athletic Department at your local school. Following Jesus can get you into trouble with other parents. Following Jesus may get you into trouble with local government, and following Jesus may even get you into trouble with other churches.

Jesus got into trouble with other churches. They tried to have Him arrested. Following Jesus may even get you into trouble with your family.

> When the Pharisees heard that the crowds were whispering such things, they and the leading priests sent Temple

guards to arrest Jesus. But Jesus told them, "I will be with you only a little longer. Then I will return to the One Who sent Me. You will search for Me but not find Me. And you cannot go where I am going."

The Jewish leaders were puzzled by this statement. "Where is He planning to go?" they asked. "Is He thinking of leaving the country and going to the Jews in other lands? Maybe He will even teach the Greeks! What does He mean when He says, 'You will search for Me but not find Me' and 'You cannot go where I am going'?"

John 7:32-36

Jesus was predicting trouble would lead to His death – He ***would*** be leaving the planet! Once again, He reveals His deity when He said he would return to the One Who sent Him. Saying He was *returning* to God obviously meant He had come from God.

Jesus knew there was trouble brewing and He knew it would eventually be His time to submit to it. I think its good to remember that following Jesus is not smooth sailing. Trouble does come. We have an enemy of our souls who tries to bring us down and render us ineffective. He tries to distract us. People can be unkind, and it may just have something to do with the fact we are friends with Jesus. Remember: Jesus risked everything for us. Jesus wants us to live on the edge, to risk in our friendships and relationships. Why don't we? Because we do not want trouble.

I say, ***"Bring on the trouble!"*** There is supposed to be trouble when you are in a war with evil. Trouble will find us. The good news is: Jesus said we would have trouble in this world **but** that to *"take heart"* because we would *"overcome the world."* With His help, we overcome trouble.

Be ready for trouble ... and when it finds you, remember to speak the truth in love. That is what Jesus did with trouble.

Day 41: Spring in Winter

John 7:37-39

All We Need

This morning I was thirsty. I was struggling with disappointment, loneliness and fatigue. I went to Jesus. I spent time with Him, I talked with Him, shared with Him, journaled to Him, opened my heart for Him to meet me. And He did. It did not mean I was all better. But I was able to rise above the blues and go through my day able to meet the needs of people God brought through my door. Since I drank deeply from His spring, I had water flowing from my heart for those that needed it this day.

> On the last day, the climax of the Festival, Jesus stood and shouted to the crowds, "Anyone who is thirsty may come to Me! Anyone who believes in Me may come and drink! For the Scriptures declare, 'Rivers of Living Water will flow from His heart.'" (When He said "Living Water," He was speaking of the Spirit Who would be given to everyone believing in Him. But the Spirit had not yet been given because Jesus had not yet entered into His glory.)
>
> **John 7:37-39**

On this last day of the Festival, the priests would march seven times around the altar, and they would draw water and pour it out. This was symbolic of the water that flowed from the rock in the wilderness to satisfy the thirst of the Israelites. Remember the story, highly significant to the Jews: God had provided water for them when Moses spoke to the rock in the desert. They were remembering God's miracle for them.

Jesus stood up at this moment and told the people that if they would drink of Him, water would flow out of their hearts instead of a rock. He is telling them God has a new miracle for them.

Water flowing is a picture of the Holy Spirit coming and living in us, satisfying our thirst for relationship, connection and acceptance. When we come to Jesus and ask Him to fill us, He enables us to then be a fountain for others. He fills us up so that we can meet all of life's disappointments, loneliness and challenges with His grace. We can flow into people's lives, ministering to their needs, being Jesus to them.

Drink deeply today. Meet with Jesus, talk with Him. Let Him fill your soul with the water of grace. His compassion is new every morning. May you have a Spring in the middle of Winter.

Day 42: Celebrating Christ or Christmas?

John 7:40-52

"Who Is Jesus?"

As I'm writing this, the snow is falling early this Christmas Eve; we are going to have a very white Christmas. Many in this *"one nation under God"* will celebrate Christmas in some fashion, but most will not celebrate Jesus. To this day, we are still divided over Who Jesus is: is He the Savior, the One Who saves us from our sins, guilt and shame? From the power of sin's grip? From being lost? From God's justifiable wrath and eternal judgment for our sin? From Satan's control over our lives? From our core selfishness? If you believe this, then you will truly celebrate Jesus this Christmas. If not, you will just celebrate Christmas.

The core question is the same as it was in this passage: *"Where is Jesus from?"* The crowds thought He was from Galilee because that is where He grew up. They knew the Scriptures, and how the Messiah was to come from Bethlehem, the city of Kings, where the great king David had been born. Most of the crowd did not know that Jesus – although He grew up in Galilee – did indeed fulfill prophecy by being born in Bethlehem.

Remember that Mary and Joseph travelled to Bethlehem to fulfill this prophecy, under the requirement of going for a census. This point of confusion for many of the people was simply they did not know where Jesus was from. Read about it:

> When the crowds heard Him say this, some of them declared, "Surely this Man is the prophet we've been expecting."
>
> Others said, "He is the Messiah."
>
> Still others said, "But He can't be! Will the Messiah come from Galilee? For the Scriptures clearly state that the Messiah will be born of the Royal Line of David, in Bethlehem, the village where King David was born." So the crowd was divided about Him. Some even wanted Him arrested, but no one laid a hand on Him.
>
> When the Temple guards returned without having arrested Jesus, the leading priests and Pharisees demanded, "Why didn't you bring Him in?"
>
> "We have never heard anyone speak like this!" the guards responded.
>
> **John 7:40-46**

Can you feel their confusion? Something in their hearts told them Jesus was for real. They saw the miracles. They heard Him speak about the Scriptures and things of Heaven like no one else. In their hearts, they knew He was God – in their heads, they just could not be convinced. We do that today. We still have a hard time wrapping our heads around what we KNOW to be true in our hearts. That is why we need FAITH. That is the whole point of FAITH.

> "Have you been led astray too?" the Pharisees mocked. "Is there a single one of us rulers or Pharisees who believes in Him? This foolish crowd follows Him but they are ignorant of the Law. God's curse is on them!"
>
> Then Nicodemus, the leader who had met with Jesus earlier, spoke up. "Is it legal to convict a man before he is given a hearing?" he asked.
>
> **John 7:47-51**

Good old Nicodemus, the real "saint Nick." Remember him? The Jewish leader who **knew in his heart** that Jesus was the real deal? He had gone in secret to meet with him at night, and Jesus had talked to him about being "born again," about letting Christ give you a new life. Most Christian scholars believe Nicodemus made the "leap of faith" – this great teacher of Jewish law joined together scriptural prophecy with biblical faith and **believed** – that is why he stood up for Jesus here.

> They replied, "Are you from Galilee too? Search the Scriptures and see for

yourself - no prophet ever comes from Galilee!"

John 7:52

So it comes down to this: where is Jesus from? Is He from Galilee, born in the right place at the right time to foster a legend, a baby in a manger? Is He only a story that just happened to not only survive over thousands of years, but thrive, capturing the hearts of millions of people? Human, like the rest of us?

Or is He from Heaven? Immanuel. God with us. The Creator and Savior of the world. Spirit-placed in a virgin girl named Mary. The Captain of the Hosts of Heaven – yet a Warrior submitted to the vulnerability of a human baby's body? One Who would defeat the power of Satan, death and Hell through His journey to the cross, the grave and resurrection? A Leader whom millions of people over time choose to live and die for?

Like the people in this story, each of us must decide for ourselves Who Jesus is. Legend from Galilee, or Holy God of Heaven?

For me, tonight is Christmas Eve, and tomorrow Christmas Day. On your next Christmas Day, will you celebrate Jesus? Or will you just celebrate Christmas?

Day 43: Jesus in a Pickle

John 8:1-11

Unfailing Friendship

The Jewish leaders were always trying to trap Jesus, to make Him look bad to everyone, to disqualify Him from being God. They found a woman who has been caught in the act of adultery, having sex with someone to whom she was not married. The Jewish Law stated that she must be stoned to death. But Jesus' message was one of grace and forgiveness, repentance and faith. They thought they had Him cornered – what would He tell them?

If He said, *"Stone her"* – which would have agreed with Law – He would have lost credibility with all the sinners He had befriended with the message of grace and forgiveness He had been giving to them. If He said, *"Do not stone her,"* then He was openly breaking the Law and subject to arrest. It seems like they had Jesus in a pickle. Here is the way it went down:

> Jesus returned to the Mount of Olives, but early the next morning He was back again at the Temple. A crowd soon gathered, and He sat down and taught them.
>
> As He was speaking, the teachers of religious law and the Pharisees brought a woman who had been caught in the act of adultery. They put her in front of the

crowd. "Teacher," they said to Jesus, "this woman was caught in the act of adultery. The Law of Moses says to stone her. What do You say?"

They were trying to trap Him into saying something they could use against Him, but Jesus stooped down and wrote in the dust with His finger. They kept demanding an answer, so He stood up again and said, "All right, but let the one who has never sinned throw the first stone!" Then He stooped down again and wrote in the dust.

John 8:1-8

No one knows what Jesus wrote on the dirt floor of the Temple. Was He simply reminding them that the Ten Commandments had been originally written *"by the finger of God"* – and that He was God? Or maybe he was exposing each one of them by writing down sins they had committed that no one knew about. Perhaps He was writing down their hidden sins, and it was better to just slip away than to be publicly exposed. Some think perhaps He was writing the name of the woman or women each potential stone-thrower had adulterous thoughts about in the hidden corner of his mind. No one knows, but the fact is ... no one stayed to throw the first stone.

When the accusers heard this, they slipped away one by one, beginning with the oldest, until only Jesus was left in

> the middle of the crowd, with the woman. Then Jesus stood up again and said to the woman, "Where are your accusers? Didn't even one of them condemn you?"
>
> "No, Lord," she said.
>
> And Jesus said, "Neither do I. Go, and sin no more."
>
> **John 8:9-11**

Jesus is so worthy of our adoration! This is one of the great reasons I adore Jesus at Christmas. He does not condemn me! He accepts me in my condition, lavishes me with grace I do not deserve, meets me in my brokenness, and then begins walking with me down the road of becoming who He wants me to be. The culture He provides is one of warm grace, not stone-cold condemnation.

That being said, Jesus is not soft on sin. Notice He did not tell the woman her sin was okay. He said to her – and says to you and me – ***"Go, and sin no more."*** He has provided us a culture in which to sin no more. What we try to find illegitimately through sin, we find legitimately in Jesus Christ, the River of Life.

What do you suppose this woman was searching for in her illegitimate relationships with men? Acceptance. Love. Sin is illegitimately trying to meet our legitimate needs that God designed to only be met in Christ. He gave us ways to legitimately meet the needs He created us with. In other words, I have needs for friendship that can be partly met with great Christian friends, with my wife, with my kids. But ultimately, my Best Friend, my unfailing friendship comes from Jesus. He is always there for me, and never lets me down.

I adore Jesus this Christmas Day for bringing grace, truth and love to this stone-cold world, and for loving me, accepting me and truthfully leading me more and more out of sin into Life.

There is another lesson here worth mentioning, for those of us who feel better when we have thrown a few stones. It is easy to throw stones at those who struggle with something that you do not. It is easy to pass judgment on someone who sins in ways you do not. Something in us feels better when we pick up a couple of rocks made of critical words, coming out of a judgmental heart, and lob them out there. There is something ugly and very selfish in each of us that loves to express, *"See, I am not **that** bad"* or *"At least I do not do **that**!"*

Jesus set the playing field straight when He said, *"If you are without **any** sin, throw the first stone."* I love that about Jesus. Even then, He was protecting you and me from condemnation that was sure to come at us, stones that would be thrown to do harm to us over the sins we have done. I adore Jesus because He brought a new plan for sin: Forgive it, overcome it, be free from it.

When you celebrate Jesus on Christmas, have fun, enjoy Him, and adore Him for bringing us grace when the Law said we each deserved death. He is worthy of our adoration today.

Merry Jesus Christ-mas!

Day 44: Being In the Light

John 8:12-20

The Greater Blaze

> Jesus spoke to the people once more and said, "I AM the Light of the world. If you follow Me, you won't have to walk in darkness because you will have the light that leads to life."
>
> **John 8:12**

Have you ever thought about what this world would be like if Jesus had not come? If the Holy Spirit was not here? If there was no presence of God on this Earth? What would it be like? It would be terribly dark.

The Holy Spirit lives in each of us, so we each bear the light of Christ. The more lights there are in one place, the greater the blaze. That is why there are still places on this Earth that are dark, spiritually speaking. Bad things happen there, like in India. Satan does horrible things through people, like the raping and setting on fire of a young girl in Orissa, leaving her for dead.

Without the Light of Christ, the Holy Spirit living in us, this world would be much like Sodom and Gomorrah was. Dark. Filled with sin. Anarchy. But we have light! We have Christ. We can see where we are, and where we are going.

When we live in Light for a long time, our eyes become accustomed to it. We get used to it. We even take it for granted. We should never take our Light for granted. We do not know what it would be like to be in total Darkness. We are blessed to be in the Light. To be led by Christ. To be led to Life. That is what Jesus said about Himself: *"I AM the Light!"*

> The Pharisees replied, "You are making those claims about Yourself! Such testimony is not valid."
>
> Jesus told them, "These claims are valid even though I make them about Myself. For I know where I came from and where I am going, but you don't know this about Me. You judge Me by human standards, but I do not judge anyone.
>
> "And if I did, My judgment would be correct in every respect because I am not alone. The Father Who sent Me is with Me. Your own Law says that if two people agree about something, their witness is accepted as fact. I am one Witness, and My Father Who sent Me is the other."

John 8:13-18

The Jews had a law that stated any important testimony needed two witnesses. So Jesus once again used their Law to make the point. He was a witness unto Himself by the miracles and healings He performed. His Father was His Witness through the Holy Scriptures, the Word of God and the fulfillment of prophecy that all confirmed Jesus as Messiah.

The Jews worked hard to understand Scripture and discern the times, so it is tragic they held in their very hands the Father's testimony of Jesus, and failed to see the truth and make the connection.

> "Where is Your Father?" they asked.
>
> Jesus answered, "Since you don't know who I am, you don't know Who My Father is. If you knew Me, you would also know My father." Jesus made these statements while He was teaching in the section of the Temple known as the Treasury. But He was not arrested because His time had not yet come.
>
> **John 8:19-20**

Once again, Jesus points out that they are in the dark about Who He is. And since they do not know Who He is, they also CANNOT know the Father. Now these Jews prided themselves on knowing the Father through the Scriptures and the teachings of Moses. But Jesus once more makes it clear that HE is the Way, the Truth and the Life. He is the Light. He reveals the glory of the Father. He shows the way to the Father. You can only know God the Father through Jesus Christ the Son.

I am glad that I know Jesus. I really do trust Him to lead me and guide me to eternal life. It is a wonderful thing to be in the Light.

Day 45: Second Chances

John 8:21-30

Citizens of Heaven

"You're too smart for your own good." That is what my mom used to say when I thought I knew better than her, or I would talk back. She would also say, *"You're too big for your britches,"* and that is sort of the same. Probably just depended on the day.

In our story today, these religious leaders were "too smart for their own good." They let their head-knowledge get in the way of their heart. They were blocked from believing in Jesus because they could not figure Him out.

We are too smart for our own good today too. *"Knowledge is king."* It is interesting that a "theory" which has never been proven – and, in fact, been largely disproven – is still taught in our public schools today. And generally believed by millions of people because they are "too smart for their own good." On that Day Jesus comes back, only one thing will matter: did you believe?

Here Jesus tells them what will happen to them if they continue being "too smart for their own good."

> Later Jesus said to them again, "I am going away. You will search for Me but will die in your sin. You cannot come where I am going."

The people asked, "Is He planning to commit suicide? What does He mean, 'You cannot come where I am going'?"

Jesus continued, "You are from Below; I am from Above. You belong to this world; I do not. That is why I said that you will die in your sins, for unless you believe that I AM Who I claim to be, you will die in your sins."

John 8:21-24

There is a change that happens when we believe: **we change citizenship.** Our citizenship is *"from Above,"* like Jesus. We are here on a temporary visa, but more and more we long to go home.

Warren Wiersbe says it well:

The true believer has his citizenship in Heaven (Luke 10:20; Philippians 3:20–21). His affection and attention are fixed Heaven-ward. But the unsaved belong to this world; in fact, Jesus called them "the children of this world" *(Luke 16:8). Since they have not trusted Christ and had their sins forgiven, their destiny is to die in their sins. The Christian dies* "in the Lord" *because he lives* "in the Lord" *(Revelation 14:13); but the unbeliever dies in his sins because he lives in his sins.*

As true believers, citizens of Heaven will find ourselves becoming less and less attached to this world as time goes by. Status, money, degrees, stuff, and where you live, will all take on less meaning. Why? Because our hearts are in Heaven with Jesus. We realize none of this brings joy, only He does. We live more for "Above" and less for "Below." Jesus went on ...

"Who are You?" they demanded.

Jesus replied, "The One I have always claimed to be. I have much to say about you and much to condemn, but I won't. For I say only what I have heard from the One Who sent Me, and He is completely truthful."

But they still didn't understand that He was talking about His Father. So Jesus said, "When you have lifted up the Son of Man on the cross, then you will understand that I AM He. I do nothing on My own but say only what the Father taught Me. And the One Who sent Me is with Me -- He has not deserted Me. For I always do what pleases Him." Then many who heard Him say these things believed in Him.

John 8:25-30

Again, Jesus uses the Name reserved by the Jews only for Almighty God: *I AM.* And finally He tells them, *"Hey, most of you are not going to get this until you have murdered Me on the cross. Then you will understand."*

What amazes me about this is God's incredible patience with people. I mean, how many chances do we get? Jesus spells it out for them, over and over, multiple times. Then He finally says, *"Okay, you will get it when I am gone. I will give you even another chance."*

I am grateful for second chances. I needed one. I took the grace of God and went and ate with the pigs for a time. And Jesus took me back. Actually, He had never left me. Now, like Jesus said, I try to do the thing that pleases Him. Because I am grateful. When I deserved judgment, He gave me amazing grace. How do you ever repay that?

Live for the Above. You are no longer from Below.

Day 46: Freedom

John 8:31-47

About Spiritual DNA

There's a story about training elephants. If from the time they are young you chain their leg to a post, then when they are old, you don't even have to stake the chain anymore. Why? Because they stay put because they think the chain is still holding them captive.

Do you know you do not have to sin? Do you know you have a choice whether to do right or do wrong? Every choice you make – whether to be loving or mean, be generous or greedy – is up to you. Jesus set you free from "having" to sin. You do not have to sin anymore.

How do you know you are free? How do you know you are no longer a slave to sin? Jesus paid for our freedom, paying the ransom for sin on the cross. We are freed by believing in Jesus, by receiving this sacrifice, right? We are saved by faith.

But how do we know? Do we not want to know that we are free? Jesus tells us ....

> Jesus said to the people who believed in Him, "You are truly My Disciples if you remain faithful to My teachings. And you will know the truth, and the truth will set you free."

"But we are descendants of Abraham," they said. "We have never been slaves to anyone. What do You mean, 'You will be set free'?"

Jesus replied, "I tell you the truth: everyone who sins is a slave of sin. A slave is not a permanent member of the family, but a son is part of the family forever. So if the Son sets you free, you are truly free."

John 8:31-36

Some people do not even realize they need freedom, they are not aware that they are slaves to sin. Some people think that if they live a pretty good life, if they are "descendants of Abraham," then they will be saved. But the truth is, anyone who depends on their own works to try to get to Heaven is still a slave to sin. That's the point – we cannot depend on our own works, we can only depend on the work Jesus did on the cross to be free. Depending on yourself **is** SIN. Self-dependence is slavery to sin.

Choosing to change our dependence over to Jesus and what He did is freedom. Jesus paid the ONLY PRICE for slavery to sin. There was only one price to buy our freedom: the sacrifice of a perfect human, God in the flesh. Only Jesus could pay it ... so try as we might, work as we might, we can never pay the price. Only the Son can set us free. True freedom is realizing and accepting Jesus' provision.

Jesus goes on to say:

"Yes, I realize that you are descendants of Abraham. And yet some of you are trying to kill Me because there's no room in your hearts for My message. I am telling you what I saw when I was with My Father. But you are following the advice of your father."

"Our father is Abraham!" they declared.

"No," Jesus replied, "for if you were really the children of Abraham, you would follow his example. Instead, you are trying to kill Me because I told you the truth, which I heard from God. Abraham never did such a thing. No, you are imitating your real father."

John 8:37-41

Here, they are trying to identify with Abraham, whom God approved of because of his faith. The problem is: this faith is not their own. It is the faith of a man who has been dead hundreds of years. You cannot be freed by another man's faith. Jesus points out that if they really were Abraham's children, they would love Jesus because Abraham loved God. The *"real father"* he refers to is Satan – that they are really children of Satan because they are contemplating murder in their hearts. Satan is a murderer. They are offended by this!

They replied, "We aren't illegitimate children! God Himself is our true Father."

Jesus told them, "If God were your Father, you would love Me because I have come to you from God. I am not here on My own, but He sent Me. Why can't you understand what I am saying? It's because you can't even hear Me! For you are the children of your father the devil, and you love to do the evil things he does. He was a murderer from the beginning. He has always hated the truth, because there is no truth in him. When he lies, it is consistent with his character for he is a liar and the father of lies. So when I tell the truth, you just naturally don't believe Me!

"Which one of you can truthfully accuse Me of sin? And since I am telling you the truth, why don't you believe Me? Anyone who belongs to God listens gladly to the words of God. But you don't listen because you don't belong to God."

John 8:41-47

Pedigree is proven by characteristics. We can tell who someone's father is because they look like him. If we can't tell by the look, we can tell by the DNA. Jesus is saying He can tell they are still slaves to sin, children of the devil, because they act like him. They lie, they contemplate murder, and they don't love God. **They have the DNA of the devil.**

People who have been freed from slavery begin to change. It comes back to what Jesus said in the beginning of this text: *"You are truly My disciples if you remain faithful to My teachings"* (verse 31).

How do we know we are not slaves anymore, that we have been freed by Jesus? We imitate our Deliverer. We become like Him. We become faithful to Jesus' teachings. We learn Who He is through His Word, like we are doing right now as we study the Gospel of John together. We learn what His characteristics are, and we submit to a process to become God's children by becoming like the Son. We have a different pedigree.

A slave represents his master. A son looks like his father. Are you a slave or an heir?

Day 47: Hearts Exposed

John 8:48-59

Caring For Others

I was sitting in the parking lot at the Seattle International Airport, waiting for my wife's plane to arrive from Taiwan. Before my eyes, I observed a woman backing up her car, trying to get a spot, and hitting the car behind her. A few words were exchanged, and the lady moved her car and parked on the side. That is when I noticed the parked driver was an old friend of mine, a young man whom I have known for years.

As I left my truck and went to say hello, the woman driver came over and immediately tried to blame my friend for being too close behind her; she said she could not see him. Things began to escalate from there, and finally I spoke up, stating I had witnessed the accident, and she was clearly at fault as her vehicle was the only one moving.

Boy, was she angry! She turned on me, said some unkind things, verbally attacking me. I was surprised. All she had to do was simply accept responsibility, and the conversation would have been quite different. Instead, knowing she was clearly in the wrong, she still tried to cover her mistake by blaming my friend. All I had done was speak the truth to try to resolve the situation. She responded to the truth by attacking me, someone she had never met and did not know.

Temperatures rise when people feel exposed. In this conversation Jesus is having with the Jewish leaders, temperatures are rising. Whenever we are confronted and exposed, our natural tendency is to defend ourselves or fight back. Jesus is loving them by speaking the truth to them, and they react by turning His words back on Him and accusing Him:

> The people retorted, "You Samaritan devil! Didn't we say all along that You were possessed by a demon?"
>
> "No," Jesus said, "I have no demon in Me. For I honor My Father - and you dishonor me. And though I have no wish to glorify Myself, God is going to glorify Me. He is the true Judge. I tell you the truth: anyone who obeys My teaching will never die! Are you greater than our Father Abraham? He died, and so did the prophets. Who do you think You are?"

John 8:48-53

People who are slaves to sin attack those who have the Spirit of God within. Sometimes we wonder why someone we do not even know is so rude to us, or even mean. Perhaps it is their connection with the Father of Lies that makes them resent us, who have the spirit of Christ living in us. I think many times when we run into issues with people it can be that we are not even wrestling with them but with the influence of sin and Satan upon their soul. Their master recognizes our Master ... and the battle is on.

So what are we to do when these battles happen? Well, what would Jesus do?

> Jesus answered, "If I want glory for Myself, it doesn't count. But it is My Father Who will glorify Me. You say, 'He is our God,' but you don't even know Him. I know Him. If I said otherwise, I would be as great a liar as you! But I do know Him, and obey Him. Your Father Abraham rejoiced as he looked forward to My coming. He saw it and was glad."
>
> The people said, "You aren't even fifty years old. How can You say You have seen Abraham?"
>
> **John 8:54-57**

Jesus spoke the truth for their benefit and to bring glory to God. He knew they were dying in their sin, and so He threw them a lifeline of truth. He did it at significant personal risk to Himself, knowing they might not receive the truth He had to offer them. So once more, Jesus tells them clearly the truth about His nature, that He is indeed God.

You see, they recognized Abraham as the father of their faith. They believed that by identifying with Abraham's faith and keeping the Laws God had given them, they could earn their way into Heaven. But Jesus adjusts their faulty, self-dependent thinking by reminding them that as God, He existed long before Abraham was even born, in Eternity Past.

> Jesus answered, "I tell you the truth: before Abraham was even born, I AM!" At that point, they picked up stones to throw at Him. But Jesus was hidden from them, and left the Temple.
>
> **John 8:58-59**

Jesus spoke the truth to them in love, and they responded by picking up stones to murder Him. It was not His time to die so He was supernaturally hidden from them. He disappeared. They could not find Him.

Sometimes people do not want to hear the Truth, but we must let them hear it. Of course, the key to speaking the Truth to someone is our motive for doing it. Are we just wanting to be right? Just wanting to win the fight? Just wanting to prove a point? Get our way? Get something we want? If so, then our motive is wrong.

The reason we speak the Truth is because we care for others, and we want to bring glory to God. The Truth we speak should clear their path toward Christ, and as they respond to the Holy Spirit – the ultimate Truth-Speaker – it will bring glory to God. We may have to dodge a few stones, we may even get abused or turned upon. But know this: God will not let us die before our time.

Relationships that are not grounded in Truth are not relationships at all. We must love people enough to speak the Truth to them, for their benefit. The best thing we could tell people is Jesus loves them. And while we are at it, show them! That way they will believe it is really true.

Day 48: Healing Today

John 9:1-13

Reality Or Fantasy?

God still heals today. I have seen Him do it with my own eyes. Read the story, and then we will share some observations about healing.

> As Jesus was walking along, He saw a man who had been blind from birth. "Rabbi," His disciples asked Him, "why was this man born blind? Was it because of his own sins or his parents' sins?"
>
> "It was not because of his sins or his parents' sins," Jesus answered. "This happened so the power of God could be seen in him. We must quickly carry out the tasks assigned us by the One Who sent us. The night is coming, and then no one can work. But while I am here in the world, I am the Light of the world."
>
> Then He spit on the ground, made mud with the saliva, and spread the mud over the blind man's eyes. He told him, "Go wash yourself in the Pool of Siloam (Siloam means 'sent'). So the man went and washed, and came back seeing!
>
> His neighbors and others who knew him as a blind beggar asked each other, "Isn't this the man who used to sit and beg?"

Some said he was, and others said, "No, he just looks like him!"

But the beggar kept saying, "Yes, I am the same one!"

They asked, "Who healed you? What happened?"

He told them, "The Man they call Jesus made mud and spread it over my eyes, and told me, 'Go to the Pool of Siloam and wash yourself.' So I went and washed, and now I can see!"

"Where is He now?" they asked.

"I don't know," he replied. Then they took the man who had been blind to the Pharisees."

John 9:1-13

(1) God does not heal everyone. This day Jesus chose one man; there were dozens, if not hundreds, left unhealed.

(2) God's purposes for leaving us unhealed are usually more important than being healed. What happens when we are left unhealed?

(a) We depend on Him more fully. Often we see people with unique challenges depend more fully on God than someone who is whole.

(b) We let Jesus use us in spite of our challenge. God's power shows up in weakness, and it brings great glory to Him as He is seen through us in spite of our challenge.

(c) God has a different perspective on healing than we do. God has an eternal perspective. In light of Eternity, how important is our physical healing?

God wants one thing more than anything for us: to have us Home with Him. Let's face it, from God's perspective, our time on Earth is a snap of the fingers. God will allow us to experience some challenges here on Earth if it means we seek Him for Eternity. Only He knows what He is accomplishing in us through our challenges, such as learning to TRUST HIM in the midst of it.

(3) God heals people for purposes other than the healing. Again, Jesus was challenging the system by healing on the Sabbath. While it was important for the man to be healed, remember there were many left unhealed. Jesus healed this man on purpose for a purpose other than just the healing itself.

(4) Sickness and disease is a result of living in a broken world. Jesus made it clear that neither the man nor his parents had done anything to bring this blindness upon himself. We live in a sin-filled world, and we are all touched by sin.

The sin-fullness of this world provides such a great contrast to the glory of Christ.

(5) Healing is for the glory of God. Healing should highlight the Healer, Jesus Christ, not the event, the person or the instrument God uses (us).

(6) Healing is not in the method. This is the third different way Jesus healed a blind person's eyes: one time by just applying spit, one time by just touching the eyes, and this time by applying clay. Jesus changed the method so that we would not focus on the "how" but rather the "Who."

(7) Living with challenges develops a longing for Heaven. We all long for healing, whether it be emotional or physical. We all have challenges we wish God would take away or smooth over. It is the presence of these challenges that turn our eyes away from this world and long for Heaven, to be in the presence of God, whole and complete for Eternity.

God wants us to Long for Him, Live for Him, and get ready to Leave for Him. Whether we get our healing or not, God wants us to believe He is good. Even when He doesn't heal us.

Let your challenge help in you a longing for Heaven. Heaven is the real life. One wretched seeker said it like this:

Is this the real life
Is this just fantasy?
Caught in a landslide
No escape from reality
Open your eyes
Look up to the skies and see ...

[*"Bohemian Rhapsody"*; written by **Freddie Mercury** (1946-1991) of *Queen;* copyright © 1975; all rights reserved.]

Day 49: Stuck In the Mud

John 9:13-23

Confronted With Truth

I live in "redneck country." That means big trucks lifted high off the ground, with mud tires and gun racks. Young guys in *Romeo* boots and *Carhartt* jackets like to take their trucks down to the river and drive through the mud and ruts. The deeper the ruts and the muddier the terrain, the more they love it.

When they drive into the High School parking lot, the more mud they have on their truck, the more manly they feel. They stand around and compare muddy tracks. Sometimes they don't make it to school because they got stuck in the mud. They believed they could make it, but they couldn't. They got stuck in the mud.

People believe what they want to believe. People believe whatever evidence they can find to support the way they want to live. They go through their entire lives stuck. This story is a great example of people staying stuck in their misbeliefs even when they are confronted with truth.

> Then they took the man who had been blind to the Pharisees, because it was on the Sabbath that Jesus had made the mud and healed him. The Pharisees asked the man all about it. So he told

them, "He put the mud over my eyes, and when I washed it away, I could see!"

Some of the Pharisees said, "This Man Jesus is not from God, for He is working on the Sabbath." Others said, "But how could an ordinary sinner do such miraculous signs?" So there was a deep division among them.

John 9:13-16

Here we have an amazing miracle, substantiated by results and testimony. A man who had been blind from birth could now see. It was the truth. It was right before their eyes. But they would not accept it, they would not believe.

It is sad what people do with truth. Truth always brings opportunity to change. Here they have the evidence right in front of them. But instead of focusing on the amazing confirmation that Jesus was indeed God – was sent by God – they chose to focus on mud. Here they had an amazing opportunity to open their hearts to truth and change, to receive a new and better way of thinking and living – and they chose to find fault with Jesus' method. They could not see past the mud. They did not want Jesus to be God; it did not work with their lifestyle. So they made mud the issue.

God had commanded Moses to have the Jews take a day of rest and keep it holy. The Jews had added lots of Man-made ideas and laws to God's

Law of keeping the Sabbath. They had made it difficult to do anything at all on the Sabbath. That is why they could not look past the mud. They were stuck in the mud. You see, according to their narrow minds, Jesus had to **work** to make the mud. He had to stir up the mud, He had to apply the mud to the man's eyes. Clearly He was working on the Sabbath! And then He had to actually perform the healing, and that was **work** too (actually, for Jesus, that was probably fun). Because of how they wanted to live, how they wanted life to work for them, they made MUD the issue. Look at the great lengths the Jewish leaders went to explain away what was right in front of them.

> Then the Pharisees again questioned the man who had been blind, and demanded, "What's your opinion about this Man Who healed you?"
>
> The man replied, "I think He must be a prophet."
>
> The Jewish leaders still refused to believe the man had been blind and could now see, so they called in his parents. They asked them "Is this your son? Was he born blind? If so, how can he now see?"
>
> His parents replied, "We know this is our son and that he was born blind, but we don't know how he can see or who

> healed him. Ask him! He is old enough to speak for himself." His parents said this because they were afraid of the Jewish leaders who had announced that anyone saying Jesus was the Messiah would be expelled from the synagogue. That's why they said, "He is old enough. Ask him."
>
> **John 9:17-23**

People believe what they want to believe. When you share truth with them, instead of receiving the truth and embracing the opportunity to change, they throw mud. People are afraid of being wrong. They bring up all the reasons why it is not their fault. They miss the truth because they focus on the mud. You might say they are stuck in the mud because they do not want to GIVE UP their system, their ways. They think it is working for them. That is what the Jews did ... and that is what people still do today.

Before we get too down on people, remember there *were* some others there that day: people who believed. People who wanted to change. People who were open to receive truth. People who were willing to say, *"You know, maybe this Jesus has something to say. Maybe He is legit. Maybe I should at least consider His words."* They were willing to ask the question, *"How could an ordinary sinner do such miraculous signs?"* I hope I would be one of these people. I think I am. I think I am open to Jesus doing what He wants in me.

That is a great question: *"Jesus, what do You want to do in me?"* Are we open to truth? Are we open to change? Are we humble enough to receive input from those closest to us? Those who know us the best? Or, when they try to "open our eyes" about ourselves, do we just focus on mud? Are we blind? Do we have a hard time seeing ourselves the way others see us?

I understand. I often wonder how people see me. Change is hard. Humility is hard. It is difficult to hear someone say, *"You could be a better person if you changed."* It is messy, it is muddy. The moment someone shares something we could change about ourselves, it seems all we can see are the things THEY need to change. We see all the mud. And it is much easier to pick up a handful of mud and sling it back than to embrace change and consider what might be true about ourselves.

Here is a concept worth considering: instead of believing what we want to believe, try being open to what Jesus says. Jesus is still opening blind eyes. Are we letting Him put mud on our eyes? Be open to God's Word. Read it. Believe it. If we do not want to believe what loved ones say, at least believe what Jesus says – and change for Him. He wants us to be the best we can be. That is the truth. Believe.

Day 50: Open Your Eyes

John 9:24-34

The Reason For Faith

Faith embraces and requires mystery. There will always be a lot we do not know about Jesus because, for now, we don't have all the facts. That is the point of faith. ~~That is what keeps the playing-field level~~. That is why a mentally-challenged person may be saved and an award-winning physicist may not. Anyone can use the faith God has given them ... but it does mean jumping into the abyss of not knowing all.

We are human beings limited to a physical existence; we think physically – Jesus is a Heavenly Being with no metaphysical restrictions. We do not understand all there is to understand – that is why we need faith. As it says in Hebrews 11:1: *"Faith is the substance of things hoped for. Faith is the evidence of things we can't even see."* But faith hangs on to what it believes to be true – and for us, that is Jesus is opening our eyes. There is revelation all around us – in us and in His Word – that there is a God and His Name is Jesus Christ.

> "I don't know whether He is a sinner," the man replied. "But I know this: I was blind, and now I can see!"
>
> **John 9:24-25**

The formerly-blind/now-seeing man admitted he did not know much about Jesus, but this he knew for sure: *"I was blind, and now I can see!"* Faith hangs on to the thing we **know** to be true and embraces the mystery of the rest.

> "But what did He do?" they asked. "How did He heal you?"
>
> "Look!" the man exclaimed. "I told you once. Didn't you listen? Why do you want to hear it again? Do you want to become His disciples too?"
>
> **John 9:26-27**

Faith makes us willing to risk the abuse of others in order to stand up for it. Jesus had done something for the now-seeing man that no one else could do, so he puts himself out there for others. He challenges others to honestly consider the proof standing before them. Jesus had opened his eyes. He could see. And Jesus would open their eyes if they would let Him.

> Then they cursed him and said, "You are His disciple, but we are disciples of Moses! We know God spoke to Moses, but we don't even know where this Man came from."
>
> **John 9:28-29**

Faith makes us stand for Jesus even when we know it is going to cost us. Things began to get worse for the now-seeing man. Here we see people doing what people always do: since they could not refute the evidence of the change in this man's life, they began to revile the man. But the now-seeing man stood firm. He did not waver. He was in danger of being cut off from all family, friends and the church, being given the status of "cursed," but still he stands up for Jesus. You see, when Jesus opens our eyes, Life is not the same for us. We see Life differently. We begin to see from an Eternal perspective. We begin to really value Jesus, and so we stand up for Him.

Not only could the now-seeing man see for the first time, but he also understood what it cost Jesus. Jesus had brought trouble upon Himself by healing this man on the Sabbath. The now-seeing man knew how angry the Pharisees were, angry enough to murder Jesus. But because Jesus had put Himself in harm's way to bring him a new life, the now-seeing man put himself out there for Jesus.

Jesus hanged for us, so we stand for Him. It cost Him, it should cost us.

> "Why, that's very strange!" the man replied. "He healed my eyes and yet you don't know Where He comes from? We know that God doesn't listen to sinners but He is ready to hear those who worship Him and do His will. Ever since the world began, no one has been able to open the eyes of someone born blind. If this Man were not from God, He couldn't have done it."

John 9:30-33

Faith believes when God reveals. God had revealed Himself in this opening of the eyes. This was a big deal miracle. The truth was that now this man, blind from birth, could see. This now-seeing man knew he was the first and only of his kind: healed from congenital blindness. Born into blindness, he could now see. **This was evidence that could not be refuted!**

The Pharisees knew that, and yet they would not believe. Faith believes the Truth and keeps it central. This man kept Truth central:

> Before I met Jesus, I could not see > my eyes have been opened > only God can open blind eyes = Jesus must be God

The Pharisees did not like that.

> "You were born a total sinner!" they answered. "Are you trying to teach us?" And they threw him out of the synagogue.
>
> **John 9:34**

Faith costs something, but it pays off in the end. The now-seeing man endured the loss of his church, his community, his friends, and his family. He was excommunicated, he lost all his relationships ... **but** he could see! And he was free! No longer would he live under the tyranny of religious bigotry. He would now be following Jesus, the Life-Giver, the Sight-Giver. He would enter into relationship with Jesus, and the pay-off would not only be seeing, but Eternal Life. It would be worth it all.

Let us contemplate all Jesus has done for us and how we respond to Him. How much value do we place on the fact that *"once we were blind, now we can see"*? This blind man was willing to take a stand for Jesus. Let us stand for Him even better than ever before.

Day 51: The Only Reasonable Response

John 9:35-41

Belief Leads to Worship

> When Jesus heard what had happened, He found the man and asked, "Do you believe in the Son of Man?"
>
> **John 9:35**

Think about this verse, because it often gets passed over in the story. Yesterday we read that this newly-seeing man got kicked out of his synagogue and cut off from his family because he stood up for Jesus, the One Who had given him sight. Now I want you to notice Jesus' response to this, because it tells us something about Jesus.

When Jesus heard the man had been kicked out of his church, **Jesus went to find him.** I am sure Jesus was busy, He had things to do. But a Good Shepherd does what His sheep need Him to do: He finds them.

When we are hurting or treated poorly by the world for standing up for Jesus, He finds us and He asks us, *"Do you believe?"* I love that about Jesus. I can count on Him always finding me when my spirits are down, when my faith is small, when I have suffered loss for His sake. He asks the question, over and over, *"Come on, Kurt, do you believe?"*

> The man answered, "Who is He, Sir? I want to believe in Him."
>
> "You have seen Him," Jesus said, "and He is speaking to you!"
>
> "Yes, Lord, I believe!" the man said. And he worshipped Jesus.
>
> **John 9:36-38**

The great beauty of this response is wonderful to me. Think of this progression of faith:

* Jesus opens our eyes
* Our faith is activated
* Jesus finds us, reveals Himself to us
* We believe
* We worship Jesus.

Belief leads to worship. If we believe in Jesus, we worship Jesus. Why? Because if we really believe Who He is – and realize just a fraction of all He has done – no other response makes sense. I am so thankful to God that He does not judge us on our response to Him. He keeps it simple for our sake. Just believe.

That being said, the more our eyes are opened, the more we see Jesus for Who He truly is, the more it evokes a response from us. The more we worship. The more we surrender our life and will to Him. I love how Paul says this:

> And so, dear brothers and sisters, I plead with you to give your bodies to God because of all He has done for you. Let them be a living and holy sacrifice – the kind He will find acceptable. This is truly the way to worship Him. Don't copy the behavior and customs of this world, but let God transform you into a new person by changing the way you think. Then you will learn to know God's will for you, which is good and pleasing and perfect.
>
> **Romans 12:1-2**

When we truly begin to understand and acknowledge all Jesus has done for us, the only reasonable response is to worship Him. Not only for what He has done, but for Who He is. When the day comes that we see Him face to face, in all His glory, the only response we will be capable of is to fall to our face in worship. The sheer weight of His glory, power, holiness, and purity will drive us to our knees, even to lie prostrate before Him. We will truly see, and **we will worship.**

> Then Jesus told him, "I entered this world to render judgment – to give sight to the blind and to show those who think they see that they are blind."
>
> Some Pharisees who were standing nearby heard Him, and asked, "Are You saying we're blind?"

> "If you were blind, you wouldn't be guilty," Jesus replied. "But you remain guilty because you claim you see."
>
> **John 9:39-41**

People who know they are blind are not the problem – the problem is with people who think they can see. People who know they are blind search for the truth of sight. They want to know the truth, so they can be set free. They are looking for Jesus because they **know** there must be more. It is the people who think there is no more, who think they have the answers, who are truly blind.

For those of us who have known Jesus since childhood, we sometimes need to remind ourselves what it would be like not to see. For someone who received their sight later in adulthood, they know the difference: it is like night and day to them. The darkness was very real, and they love walking in the Light. And they are grateful.

If you, like me, received sight when you were very young, spend some time imagining not having Jesus in your life. How hopeless Life would be. How dark it would be without Him. When you get a feel for that darkness, then let gratefulness for your sight drive you to worship Him.

Worship Jesus! It is the only reasonable response to being able to see. See Jesus for Who He is. Worship Him.

Day 52: *"Coming and Going Freely"*

John 10:1-10

Joining With Jesus

As we read this story, keep in mind the context of what has just happened:

(1) Jesus has just healed a blind man;
(2) The now-seeing man gets rejected from the Jewish "flock" by his "shepherds," the Jewish leaders;
(3) Jesus the Good Shepherd finds the man and invites him into His flock;
(4) The now-seeing man responds to Jesus' voice and joins Jesus' flock;
(5) Jesus leads the now-seeing man into a new life of sight, faith and security.

Let's read:

"I tell you the truth: anyone who sneaks over the wall of a sheepfold rather than going through the gate must surely be a thief and a robber! But the one who enters through the gate is the shepherd of the sheep. The gatekeeper opens the gate for him, and the sheep recognize his voice and come to him.

"He calls his own sheep by name and leads them out. After he has gathered his own flock, he walks ahead of them, and they follow him because they know his voice. They won't follow a stranger; they will run from him because they don't know his voice."

John 10:1-5

Jesus is telling the Jews that He is the Good Shepherd Who will call His sheep and they will follow Him. This blind man was one example of millions who have heard His voice and followed Him. Jesus is saying, *"I am gathering My flock. My sheep are those who will respond to the Truth and will follow Me."*

In this story, Israel is the sheepfold, the Pharisees are the bad shepherds, and the blind man is one of the sheep who has run from them to the Good Shepherd. He was one of the many who had been exploited and abused by his own "shepherds."

The Jewish religious leaders had not loved and cared for the sheep; rather they had used them to provide for themselves by taking advantage of them. They had "fleeced their sheep." This now-seeing man is just one of the many sheep who would leave the fold of Judaism and join the flock of Jesus Christ the Messiah.

The story continues:

Those who heard Jesus use this illustration didn't understand what He meant, so He explained it to them: "I tell you the truth: I am the Gate for the sheep. All who came before Me were thieves and robbers. But the true sheep did not listen to them. Yes, I am the Gate. Those who come in through Me will be saved. They will come and go freely, and find good pastures. The thief's purpose is to steal and kill and destroy. My purpose is to give them a rich and satisfying life."

John 10:6-10

Jesus develops the illustration even further, and now the Good Shepherd becomes the Gate to the sheep-fold. In the shepherding days, the sheep would be put in a corral made of stone and debris. There was only one opening in the wall, and at night a good shepherd would lay across that opening to protect the sheep from those who would steal them. With his own body, he would protect them from wild animals which would come to kill and devour them. He would also keep the sheep from wandering out into the night and getting lost. A good shepherd literally WAS the GATE, the only WAY in and out of the safety of the fold.

The Jewish religious leaders would never have been the gate. They would never have given their lives for the sheep. The sheep were not safe in their care. Israel had been a sheep-fold with no gate and no good shepherd. For the first time, there would be not just a fold, but a True Flock with a True Good Shepherd. Jesus is the Gate through which every sheep who will be His must pass in order to reach the safety of the fold and become one of His own flock.

I love this statement Jesus made in verse 9b: *"They will come and go freely, and will find good pastures."* Once we are part of Jesus' flock by recognizing Him as our Good Shepherd and the only Gate to the Flock of God, we are safe. We are saved. We live out our lives on this Earth with NO FEAR! We are not prisoners of stone and debris – we are part of a flock that is **led** into pastures of rich and satisfying living. He has good things for us. The Good Shepherd wants us to feed on the rich pastures of significant living, loving and lasting relationships and eternal hope. We are free from the bondage of sin and fear. Free to *"come and go freely"* in the *"abundant life"* the Good Shepherd has provided for us.

Once we place our lives under the safety of the Good Shepherd, the thief cannot steal us or harm us in any way. Oh, the thief may **attempt** to damage us by hurting our temporary, physical bodies, **but he cannot touch our souls.** We are safe. We come and go under the care of the Good Shepherd. Our souls are safe. There is no fear. We understand that, at the end of the day, our lives are safe in His fold. This is what it means to be free, to be part of His Flock.

Here is the question to consider: into what green pastures of significance is your Good Shepherd leading you this year? In His Flock, living is giving. How does He want you to find significance through **giving yourself** away, through meaningful ministry this year?

When we become part of His Flock, grazing is serving. We eat and become full and satisfied on the pastures of significant serving. Abundant living is abundant giving. What good things does the Good Shepherd want to do with you this year? Have fun *"coming and going freely"* and *"finding those good pastures"!*

Day 53: The Good Shepherd

John 10:11-21

Jesus Knows Me

> "I AM the Good Shepherd. The Good Shepherd sacrifices His life for the sheep. A hired hand will run when he sees a wolf coming. He will abandon the sheep because they don't belong to him and he isn't their shepherd. And so the wolf attacks them and scatters the flock. The hired hand runs away because he's working only for the money and doesn't really care about the sheep."
>
> **John 10:11-13**

We follow the Good Shepherd because He lays down His life for His sheep. He lays across the entry to the fold, and lets in every sheep that is His and keeps out any impostors. Satan was prowling around like a roaring lion, seeking sheep to devour ... and Jesus, the Good Shepherd, took the attacks, brutality and death on His own body so that we, the sheep could live and be saved. He is the Way into the Fold. We get in only through Him.

For the fourth time, Jesus uses the title *"I AM"* to describe Himself. Remember, *"I AM"* was the term God used to describe Himself to Moses; the Jews reserved this title only for God. Jesus was once again referring to Himself as God.

> "I AM the Good Shepherd; I know My own sheep and they know Me, just as My Father knows Me and I know the Father. So I sacrifice My life for the sheep."
>
> **John 10:14-15**

We follow the Good Shepherd because He knows us, His sheep. This word "know" speaks of an intimate connection between God and us. He knows us all deeply and intimately. He knows how we feel about everything that happens in our lives. He knows what makes us afraid, what makes us feel valued, what makes us feel significant. He knows our needs, so He knows where to lead us to feed us. He knows our natures, and the motive behind every decision we make and every word we speak.

As we become accustomed to His voice, we get to know Him more intimately also. Our faith is developed, we trust when we hear Him call. We trust when we sense His leading. We trust when He leads us down a treacherous, steep trail because we know there will be peaceful pastures beyond. We know He will not let us fall in an abyss. We know His Voice.

> "I have other sheep too that are not in this sheepfold. I must bring them also. They will listen to My voice, and there will be one flock with one Shepherd."
>
> **John 10:16**

We follow the Good Shepherd because He loves us, the *"other sheep."* The "other sheep" Jesus is referring to are the Gentiles – us, anyone who is not Jewish. Remember: in this passage, He is speaking to the Jews and the sheepfold He refers to is Judaism. Now the Good Shepherd tells the Jews there are other sheep that He will be bringing into the One Flock of His Heavenly Father. Jews will be joined with Gentiles across all time and geography.

We will be One with all believers who ever walked the face of the Earth. We will be joined intimately to people like Peter, Paul and Mary, Martin Luther, men and women we have only read about we will be a part. Amazing! And we will be joined together into one Flock with One Good Shepherd.

> "The Father loves Me because I sacrifice My life so I may take it back again. No one can take My life from Me. I sacrifice it voluntarily. For I have the authority to lay it down when I want to and also to take it up again. For this is what My Father has commanded."
>
> **John 10:17-18**

We follow the Good Shepherd because He is indispensable. He cannot be defeated. Jesus, after laying down His life, has the power to take His life back again. Notice again this is voluntary on Jesus' part. He laid down His life for us because He loves us. We have value to Him.

Because He died for us, we belong to Him. We follow Him because who would not want to follow a Shepherd Who would lay down His life for us!

It is comforting to know that the Shepherd of our lives, the Leader of our lives, has the compassion to lay down His life for us ... and the power to take His life back again from the enemy of our souls! No one can take His life from Him – He gave it up. He took it back. It is great to follow a Good Shepherd!

> When He said these things, the people were again divided in their opinions about Him. Some said, "He's demon-possessed and out of His mind. Why listen to a Man like that?"
>
> Others said, "This doesn't sound like a man possessed by a demon! Can a demon open the eyes of the blind?"
>
> **John 10:19-21**

Truth always brings about **choice**. Sheep choose the Good Shepherd – goats choose their own way. Goats are independent. They want to roam freely and run their own lives. They do not want to be in a flock. Goats cannot be shepherded because they are not sheep.

Sheep want to be herded, tended, loved, led. Sheep will go where the Good Shepherd leads them. They will feed where the Good Shepherd finds pasture. They will learn to love other sheep in the flock. They trust their Good Shepherd. They know His voice. He knows their names.

In the words of Tommy Walker:

I have a Maker
He formed my heart
Before even Time began
My life was in His hands

He knows my name
He knows my every thought
He sees each tear that falls
And hears me when I call

I have a Father
He calls me His own
He'll never leave me
No matter where I roam

He knows my name
He knows my every thought
He sees each tear that falls
And hears me when I call.

Day 54: Choosing or Being Chosen?

John 10:22-33

Those Who Will Come

What comes first: the chicken or the egg? I remember thinking about that as a child, thinking so hard that my head hurt. Of course, now we know the answer: God created the chicken **with** the egg inside, right? Read on as we think about what comes first – believing, or being chosen to believe:

> It was now winter, and Jesus was in Jerusalem at the time of Hanukkah, the Festival of Dedication. He was in the Temple, walking through the section known as Solomon's Colonnade. The people surrounded Him and asked, "How long are You going to keep us in suspense? If You are the Messiah, tell us plainly."
>
> Jesus replied, "I have already told you, and you don't believe Me. The proof is in the work I do in My Father's Name. But you don't believe Me because you are not My sheep. My sheep listen to My voice; I know them, and they follow Me. I give them Eternal Life, and they will never perish. No one can snatch them away from Me, for My Father has given them to Me and He is more powerful

than anyone else. No one can snatch them from the Father's hand.

John 10:22-29

Why is it that some people follow Jesus and some do not? Does everyone have an equal chance to respond to truth? Are some people predisposed to choose God?

Two thieves were hanging on a cross; one cursed God and died, and the other asked Jesus to remember him. Why? Why does not everyone choose to follow the Good Shepherd? Do we choose to follow Jesus ... or are we chosen to follow Jesus? Or is it both? Is it a mysterious combination we are not meant to understand? Or is it a matter of perspective?

Read what Warren Wiersbe says:

From the human standpoint, we become His sheep by believing; but from the Divine standpoint, we believe because we are His sheep. There is a mystery here that we cannot fathom or explain, but we can accept it and rejoice (see Romans 11:33-36). God has His sheep and He knows who they are. They will hear His voice and respond.

Jesus says in verse 27: *"You don't believe because you are not My sheep."* So if we do not believe unless we are His sheep, how do we become His sheep so that we can believe? And conversely, if we are His sheep, do we choose to believe? Can we say “No” to following the Good Shepherd?

Wiersbe continues:

The lost sinner who hears God’s Word knows nothing about Divine Election. He hears only that Christ died for the sins of the world, and that he may receive the gift of Eternal Life by trusting the Savior. When he trusts the Savior, he becomes a member of God’s Family and a sheep in the Flock. Then he learns that he was “chosen ... in Him [Christ] before the foundation of the world” *(see Ephesians 1:4). He also learns that each saved sinner is the Father’s* “love gift” *to His Son (see John 10:29; 17:2, 6, 9, 11–12, 24).*

So, has the Father given every person ever born to the Son through the power of redemption? Is it a matter of **potential**: that every person born is a potential gift to the Son, and all we have to do is activate the gift by believing? Or, within the sea of humanity, are there those the Father has picked out to give as a “love gift” to the Son? No one can explain the interaction between choosing and being chosen. The Bible supports both.

Wiersbe says: *“In the Bible, Divine Election and human responsibility are perfectly balanced; and what God has joined together, we must not put asunder.”*

The real answer to this is that no one fully understands the mystery of Man's choosing God and God choosing Man. When I think about this, my head begins to hurt ... so I tend to go back to the first verse I memorized as a child: John 3:16, *"For God so loved the world that He gave His only begotten Son, that whosoever believes in Him should not perish, but have eternal life."*

I love the *"whosoever"* part of this verse, and I tend to believe God is a *"whosoever"* God. I do not understand the mystery and interaction between my choosing God and being chosen by God, but I do believe God extends the opportunity to all men to choose Him, to follow the Good Shepherd.

At the same time, I am deeply aware that, outside of Christ, there is nothing good in me. I am not good enough to make a good choice to follow the Good Shepherd. I rely entirely on the belief that a gracious ***God graciously draws me***, a disobedient child. Like the Prodigal, we choose to leave the pig trough of Life and go home. We choose, yet are drawn by the love of a Father. Which has the more power? Going home to His love and acceptance is the only thing that makes sense. Could we choose to stay away? As for me, I do not want to find that out!

It says in Romans 11:32 that God has bound every person over to disobedience so that He may have mercy on us all. So I simply accept what I do not understand, and trust that God is really a Good

Shepherd and will bring every sheep who will come into the fold possible. He knows the thoughts, intentions and condition of every sheep's heart, and will be entirely just with every one. Part of faith is embracing and accepting the mystery of what we do not fully understand. Just be grateful as I am that you are one of His sheep. No one can steal you from the Good Shepherd.

At the end of the day, it is not about us – it is about the Glory of God. Jesus goes on to bring it home:

> "The Father and I are One." Once again the people picked up stones to kill Him. Jesus said, "At My Father's direction I have done many good works. For which one are you going to stone Me?"
>
> They replied, "We're stoning You not for any good work but for blasphemy! You, a mere man, claim to be God."
>
> **John 10:30-33**

It is really all about God! Finally Jesus gives them the clear answer they are looking for. He is nearing the cross, and He becomes increasingly bold with His confession. The language Jesus uses here, being "one" with the Father, clearly identifies Him as God.

To the Jewish leaders, since they did not believe Him, this was blasphemy and punishable under Jewish law by death.

Could the Jewish leaders have believed Jesus? He gave them miracles to help them believe ... He gave scriptural evidence of Himself to help them believe ... He invited them to believe. And some, like Nicodemus, did believe. And some like Paul – after Jesus' death and resurrection – would believe. Choosing or being chosen ... ah, the wonderful mystery of the Mysterious God!

Day 55: Following God's Timing

John 10:34-42

A Bit of Heaven On Earth

I love playing music "in the groove." It is so satisfying as a musician when you hit that perfect timing with the drums and the bass, you lock into the tempo, and you are "in the groove." It is at that moment you become one with the music, and one with the other players. Musically, it is a little bit of Heaven on Earth.

God's timing is perfect when our lives are in His hand. When we are trusting Him for His provision and guidance, we can count on His timing. When we desire to have His will accomplished in our lives, we can have rest and peace in our hearts. Even though circumstances may seem beyond our control and it may feel like God is not active, we have peace knowing we are in His hand because we are seeking Him and trusting Him. Remember: Jesus was following God's timing, and people were trying to kill Him wherever He went. Isn't that encouraging?

> Jesus replied, "It is written in your own Scriptures that God said to certain leaders of the people, 'I say, you are god!' And you know that the Scriptures cannot be altered. So if those people who received God's message were called 'gods,' why do you call it blasphemy

when I say, 'I AM the Son of God'? After all, the Father set Me apart and sent Me into the world.

"Don't believe Me unless I carry out My Father's work. But if I do His work, believe in the evidence of the miraculous works I have done, even if you don't believe Me. Then you will know and understand that the Father is in Me and I am in the Father."

Once again, they tried to arrest Him, but He got away and left them. He went beyond the Jordan River near the place where John was baptizing and stayed there awhile. "John didn't perform miraculous signs," they remarked to one another, "but everything he said about this Man has come true." And many who were there believed in Jesus.

John 10:34-42

This is the last time Jesus would visit Jerusalem until Palm Sunday. He was on the Father's timetable. He was listening to the Father to live out His days in God's timing, and He discerned the time was not right to be captured and killed. They tried to take Him, but He supernaturally eluded them and got away. He had tried everything to get them to believe, but they were resistant. Now He went to where God led Him. Notice what happened when He did: many believed in Him.

It is important to remember what the main thing is and stay focused upon it. **The main thing is people coming to Christ.** The main thing is not where we live, what we do for a career, or even who we marry. The main thing is people coming to Christ. Wherever we go, whatever we do, we want to be a part of *"people believed in Jesus."*

There is only one thing in this world that will outlast this world, and therefore the only thing worth investing in: people. The immortal souls of people. The eternity of people. That is what God's timing is all about. That is what God's will is all about. Loving God and loving people. Helping people *"believe in Him."*

Jesus left Jerusalem. The Holy City. The great Temple. Some might have said He had been downsized to go live in the wilderness by a river. Less people, less crowds. But it was God's timing. And people believed.

Wherever you are today – at home with your kids ... at work ... at the unemployment office ... looking for a job ... going to the store ... at school ... talking with your spouse – remember that if you are following God, you are in His timing, and He has something for you there. Redeem the time, use it well. Speak life into the lives we are around. Wherever there are people, there is purpose. People need to believe in Jesus. Help them believe.

Day 56: When God Delays

John 11:1-16

A Different Measurement of Time

Ever notice that God's timing is different than ours? The Apostle Peter said that, to God, *"a day is as a thousand years."* Sometimes it feels like a thousand years when we are waiting for God to answer a prayer, or help get us out of trouble. When we are waiting for God, it can feel like He is just taking His time.

> A man named Lazarus was sick. He lived in Bethany with his sisters, Mary and Martha. This is the Mary who later poured the expensive perfume on the Lord's feet and wiped them with her hair. Her brother Lazarus was sick, so the two sisters sent a message to Jesus, telling him, "Lord, Your dear friend is very sick."
>
> But when Jesus heard about it, He said, "Lazarus' sickness will not end in death. No, it happened for the glory of God so that the Son of God will receive glory from this." So although Jesus loved Martha, Mary and Lazarus, He stayed where He was for the next two days. Finally He said to His disciples, "Let's go back to Judaea."
>
> But His disciples objected. "Rabbi," they said, "only a few days ago the people in

Judaea were trying to stone You. Are You going there again?"

Jesus replied, "There are twelve hours of daylight every day. During the day people can walk safely. They can see because they have the light of this world. But at night there is danger of stumbling because they have no light." Then He said, "Our friend Lazarus has fallen asleep, but now I will go and wake him up."

The disciples said, "Lord, if he is sleeping, he will soon get better!" They thought Jesus meant Lazarus was simply sleeping, but Jesus meant Lazarus had died.

So He told them plainly, "Lazarus is dead. And for your sakes, I'm glad I wasn't there, for now you will really believe. Come, let's go see him."

Thomas, nicknamed the Twin, said to his fellow disciples, "Let's go too - and die with Jesus."

John 11:1-16

Wouldn't you agree dead is too late? When someone or something is dead, we would say it is "beyond hope." Lazarus was probably already dead by the time the messenger reached Jesus. Most people would drop everything and go immediately to tend to the emergency ... but Jesus delayed. He stayed where He was. He waited. He was on the Father's timetable, and He waited until the Father said, "Go!"

Some people might say this was uncaring of Jesus. Some might say He was not sensitive to the needs of His friends. Some might say He did not show up when He should have. But Jesus said, *"It happened for the glory of God so that the Son of God will receive glory from this."*

The glory of God. This is the key to the mystery of God's timing. Whenever I am in an uncomfortable place, or I am helping someone else negotiate through a difficult time, I try to ask the question: *"God, what are You up to? What are You working on through this? How will You receive glory in this?"*

The problem is: most people do not want to think about God's glory when they are in the squeeze. We just want to be free of the squeeze. We want Jesus to show up and take away the pain, the disappointment, the discomfort. And often, He does not. At least not when we think He should.

It is not that He does not love us. Lazarus, Mary and Martha were some of Jesus' closest friends. He loved them dearly. The fact is, Jesus loves us more than we love ourselves. That is the other key. He sees the bigger picture of perfecting us, not pacifying us.

When God delays showing up in our lives, it is always about three things: (a) for His glory and the glory of the Son; (b) for our perfection; and (c) helping us put our trust in Him, depending on Him. He loves us so much He will allow Himself to appear uncaring in the eyes of the world so that we become more perfect in Him.

How does He do this? What is happening while He delays?

(1) **Dependence on Him** – Waiting on Him brings us to the end of ourselves, our self-reliance, and makes us more dependent on Him. We only become dependent on Him when we find ourselves in situations that are beyond hope. We learn to pray our way through. God wants us fully dependent on Him.

(2) **Perfection in our character** – As we face discomfort time after time, He is working flaws out of our character. We learn to respond in ways that show we are convinced of His goodness and love. Eventually we come to the realization that it does not help to become angry, frustrated, depressed, or blaming. We learn to embrace disappointment and cast our every care upon Him because He cares for us, and still care for others.

(3) **Deeper faith in God** and unwavering belief that He is Good, regardless of our circumstances – Wasn't that the deal with Job? Wasn't it Satan's goal to get Job to speak ill of

God? Didn't Job's wife even tell Job in the midst of His excruciating pain to curse God and die? God wants us to trust Him and believe He is good even when it seems our circumstances tell another story.

Again, its so important to remember that comfort in this Life is not the goal of God, and should not be ours either. For many Christians around the world, discomfort is their reality. They have learned to trust God in the midst of it.

When God delays, our goal is to discern what He is up to in our lives and the lives of others, and cooperate with Him. Our goal is to trust in Him. Our goal is to see that He gets glory for what He does in our circumstances, and to come to the place that – should the worse thing happen to us – we know that He is good, it will be over soon and we will be with Him forever.

It is all about His Glory.

Day 57: When God Weeps

John 11:17-14

"Acquainted With Grief"

I loved the *"Peanuts"* comic strip when I was a kid. Every Sunday morning, I would rush to get the comics section from the Sunday newspaper, and see just what Charlie Brown, Lucy, Snoopy, Schroeder, Linus, and Pigpen were up to this week. Whenever Lucy was frustrated with Chuck, she would say, *"Good grief, Charlie Brown!"*

Really, Lucy, can grief be good?

As I have gotten older, I have realized that grief is good, in a way. When we have lost someone, when we are hurting, it is grief that opens our hearts wide to the presence of the Holy Spirit. It is in our grief that we experience the closeness and comfort like no other time. It is as if God is weeping with us, which should not surprise us since Isaiah said Jesus is *"a Man of sorrows, acquainted with the deepest grief"* (Isaiah 53:3).

When Jesus arrived at Bethany, He was told that Lazarus had already been in his grave for four days. Bethany was only a few miles down the road from Jerusalem, and many of the people had come to console Martha and Mary in their loss.

When Martha got word that Jesus was coming, she went to meet Him. But

> Mary stayed in the house. Martha said to Jesus, "Lord, if only You had been here, my brother would not have died. But even now I know that God will give You whatever You ask."
>
> Jesus told her, "Your brother will rise again."
>
> "Yes," Martha said, "he will rise when everyone else rises, at the Last Day."
>
> Jesus told her, "I AM the Resurrection and the Life. Anyone who believes in Me will live, even after dying. Everyone who lives in Me and believes in Me will never die. Do you believe this, Martha?"
>
> **John 11:17-26**

We must pause to take note of Jesus' fifth *"I AM"* statement: *"I AM the Resurrection and the Life."* From Jesus' perspective, Lazarus had already gone to Eternity. He was in a better place. Jesus knew for a fact what we all know as hope: that for those who believe in Him, Death is but a doorway into Life. Because **HE is** the Resurrection and the Life.

> "Yes, Lord," she told Him, "I have always believed You are the Messiah, the Son of God, the One Who has come into the world from God."

Then she returned to Mary. She called Mary aside from the mourners and told her, "The Teacher is here and wants to see you." So Mary immediately went to Him. Jesus had stayed outside the village, at the place where Martha met Him. When the people who were at the house consoling Mary saw her leave so hastily, they assumed she was going to Lazarus' grave to weep. So they followed here there.

When Mary arrived and saw Jesus, she fell at His feet and said, "Lord, if only You had been here, my brother would not have died."

When Jesus saw her weeping, and saw the other people wailing with her, a deep anger welled up within Him and He was deeply troubled. "Where have you put him?" He asked them.

They told Him, "Lord, come and see." Then Jesus wept.

The people who were standing nearby said, "See how much He loved him!"

But some said, "This Man healed a blind man. Couldn't He have kept Lazarus from dying?"

Jesus was still angry as He arrived at the tomb, a cave with a stone rolled across its entrance. "Roll the stone aside," Jesus told them.

But Martha, the dead man's sister, protested, "Lord, he has been dead for four days. The smell will be terrible."

Jesus responded, "Didn't I tell you that you would see God's glory if you believe?" So they rolled the stone aside. Then Jesus looked up to Heaven and said, "Father, thank You for hearing Me. You always hear Me, but I said it out loud for the sake of all these people standing here, so that they will believe You sent Me."

Then Jesus shouted, "Lazarus, come out!" And the dead man came out, his hands and feet bound in grave-clothes, his face wrapped in a head-cloth. Jesus told them, "Unwrap him and let him go."

John 11:27-44

Have you ever known a secret – some good news, something exciting – no one else knew? Like finding out your wife is pregnant? Exciting, joyful news that bubbles up inside you. Or hearing that someone who was feared to have cancer does not: it is a benign, operable tumor. You cannot wait to tell people the good news!

Jesus knew something no one else knew. He had wonderful news. Yet, Jesus wept ... and He was angry. He knew Lazarus was going to be brought back to life, yet He was grieving. Why did God weep? Perhaps ...

(1) He wept at the ravages of sin in His created world. He saw the effects of sin, and knew it was not meant to be this way – and that broke His heart.
(2) He wept at how Satan was using the fear of Death as such a weapon to keep people in bondage. To keep them under his grip.
(3) He wept because of the sorrow of His friends. Being the perfect God-man, He entered into the emotion of grief like no other. He feels and carries our sorrow like no one else can.
(4) He wept at the idea of calling his friend back from his resting place. Why would anyone want to die twice?
(5) He wept at their unbelief. Remember, He wept another time: over Jerusalem when they would not recognize, believe and receive their Creator and Messiah.

God weeps because God **feels.** It is so important that we remember He is a feeling, caring, loving God. When we go through disappointments and struggles, we often wonder where God is and what He is doing. I believe He is caring, loving and present in our pain. Just because we hurt or someone we love dies does not mean God does not see and care. He sees ...

and He enters our pain and feels our hurts.

God created us with emotion because He **has** emotion. We are created in His image. It is important, in the middle of disappointment and pain, that we see Him hurting with us. Caring about us. Weeping for us.

The writer of the book of Hebrews reminds us that Jesus is a Friend Who cares. He was a friend of Lazarus, Mary and Martha who cared deeply about their condition and what they were going through. He is our Friend Who cares deeply about what we face:

> So then, since we have a great High Priest Who has entered Heaven, Jesus the Son of God, let us hold firmly to what we believe. This High Priest of ours understands our weaknesses, for He faces all of the same testings we do yet He did not sin. So let us come boldly to the Throne of our gracious God. There we will receive His mercy, and we will find grace to help us when we need it most.
>
> **Hebrews 4:14-16**

Jesus is present with us and is caring for us in every detail of our day. Come boldly to Him. Ask for His help. He will give exactly what He knows you need. He cares for you. God weeps.

Day 58: Setting the Stage

John 11:34-57

Witnessing the Impossible

Let us imagine we are at a funeral. The casket is open and Uncle Ned is lying there, clearly dead, his body prepared for burial. The room is quiet, with some soft funeral music playing in the background. A few sniffles an be heard.

There is a rustle at the back of the room, and in comes a friend of the family from California. He walks to the casket, takes hold of Ned's cold hand, pulls him up and out of the casket, stabilizes him on his feet, and they embrace with a big back-slapping hug.

You would think when someone gets raised from the dead, it might be good proof that Jesus is pretty special! At the very least, He was a Man of God Who should be respected; at the most, He was the Messiah sent by God to fulfill His plan and His prophesy.

Many did believe Jesus was Messiah after He raised Lazarus from the dead ... but not the religious leaders. It made them even more resolved to get rid of Jesus, this "upstart" Who was edging in on their territory. More and more people were believing in Him, and they became more set that something must be done to stop Him.

> Many of the people who were with Mary believed in Jesus when they saw this

> happen. But some went to the Pharisees and told them what Jesus had done. Then the leading priests and Pharisees called the High Council together. "What are we going to do?" they asked each other. "This Man certainly performs many miraculous signs. If we allow Him to go on like this, soon everyone will believe in Him. Then the Roman Army will come, and destroy both our Temple and our nation."
>
> **John 11:45-48**

The religious leaders were thinking "earthly kingdom" while Jesus had come to bring the "Heavenly Kingdom." They were worried about the Roman soldiers, while Jesus was fighting Satan's armies of Hell. Jesus had just proven His power over Death and the grave, over Satan ... and they missed the entire point of this powerful display of God's power. They were worried about competition.

> Caiaphas, who was High Priest at that time, said, "You don't know what you're talking about! You don't realize that it's better for you that one Man should die for the people than for the whole nation to be destroyed."
>
> He did not say this on his own; as High Priest at that time, he was led to prophesy that Jesus would die for the entire nation. And not only for the

> nation, but to bring together and unite all the children of God scattered around the world.
>
> **John 11:49-52**

It is at this moment we realize the cast has been chosen, the script has been written, and the actors are on cue. Here is the irony of it: Caiaphas, the High Priest – vehemently opposed to Jesus – thinks he is saying, *"We need to kill Jesus so that the Romans will not do away with the Jews and the Temple."* However, unknowingly he is following another script: the God-script. God has Caiaphas – the enemy of Jesus – literally prophesy about the Greatest Plan of All Time: the plan of God to save the whole world! He wanted Jesus killed to save his nation; God was ordaining Jesus' death to save all of Mankind. It is clear that God is in control of this play. Awesome. Watch as the plot develops ...

> So from that time on, the Jewish leaders began to plot Jesus' death. As a result, Jesus stopped His public ministry among the people and left Jerusalem. He went to a place near the wilderness, to the village of Ephraim, and stayed there with His disciples.
>
> **John 11:53-54**

Have you ever been to a great stage-play? I mean, a really good play, maybe a murder mystery where you enjoy a few scenes, and then it is time for the last scene when the plot is going to be revealed. The curtain goes down, you sit in the dim light. There is a quiet buzz in the crowd as anticipation builds, the orchestra shifts their music around, getting ready. A few of them tune for the final scene of the play. You can feel the tension begin to build as the cast prepares for the final scene.

That is how we must read this passage. The final preparation before the final scene. There is a buzz in the crowd. The timing is right. The end is near. People are planning, talking, wondering, anticipating. The star of the play has gone to his dressing room to prepare for the final scene. He will not enter the stage prematurely … the timing will be perfect. The stage is set ....

> It was now almost time for the Jewish Passover celebration, and many people from all over the country arrived in Jerusalem several days early so they could go through the purification ceremony before Passover began. They kept looking for Jesus, but as they stood around in the Temple, they said to each other, "What do you think? He won't come for Passover, will He?"
>
> Meanwhile, the leading priests and Pharisees had publicly ordered that anyone seeing Jesus must report it immediately, so they could arrest Him.
>
> **John 11:55-57**

People all over the known world have heard of this Jesus. They are coming in crowds to Jerusalem, the City of Kings, to celebrate Passover – but also to catch a glimpse of this famous Man. Jesus knows the perfect timing of His entrance, so He stays away from the crowd. The timing will be right ... the moment will be perfect for prophesy to be fulfilled ... and the greatest Passover Sacrifice of all time to be made. The Master Playwright is in control ... the timing will be perfect ... the stage is set for the greatest drama of all time.

Day 59: God's Last Days

John 12:1-11

Being With the People We Love

If you knew you were dying, where would you want to spend your last days? I would want to be surrounded by people I love, people who know me deeply, people who will let me be myself. I would want to be with people who love me.

> Six days before the Passover Celebration began, Jesus arrived in Bethany, the home of Lazarus - the man He had raised from the dead. A dinner was prepared in Jesus' honor. Martha served, and Lazarus was among those who ate with Him.
>
> Then Mary took a twelve-ounce jar of expensive perfume made from the essence of nard, and she anointed Jesus' feet with it, wiping His feet with her hair. The house was filled with the fragrance.
>
> But Judas Iscariot, the disciple who would soon betray Him, said, "That perfume was worth a year's wages. It should have been sold and the money given to the poor." Not that he cared for the poor - he was a thief, and since he was in charge of the disciples' money, he often stole some for himself.

> Jesus replied, "Leave her alone. She did this in preparation for My burial. You will always have the poor among you, but you will not always have Me."
>
> When all the people heard of Jesus' arrival, they flocked to see Him, and also to see Lazarus, the man Jesus had raised from the dead. Then the leading priests decided to kill Lazarus too, for it was because of him that many of the people had deserted them and believed in Jesus.
>
> **John 12:1-11**

You might think God would spend His last days in the Temple. But Jesus went back to Bethany, to the place He felt most understood and accepted, and prepared Himself for the final drama. He soaked in the fellowship and community of people who were devoted to Him. One person in particular gave herself extravagantly in worship to Jesus, and Jesus received it and defended her for it. What was it about the way Mary worshipped Jesus that was so special?

(1) She was thoughtful about Jesus. Mary had sat at His feet and really listened to Him as He shared about who He was, why He was here, and what would happen to Him. She understood the heart of her Savior, and worshiped Him out of that understanding. **She anointed Him on purpose for a purpose:** she was preparing Him for His burial. Her

worship was a response to her understanding of Who He was, why He had come, and what He was about to do. True worship involves thoughtful response.

(2) She did not let the fear of Man stop her. Not everyone in the room understood what she did or why she did it. She did it anyway. She risked misunderstanding and ridicule because she loved Jesus deeply and was deeply devoted to Him. She was showing her devotion to Jesus before it was too late. She was "giving the roses" while He was yet alive, and not bringing them to the funeral! Her act of love and worship was public, spontaneous, sacrificial, lavish, unembarrassed, and personal. **True worship risks what others may think of you.**

(3) Her worship came from a heart of gratefulness and devotion. She loved Jesus because He loved and accepted her. She loved Jesus because He had forgiven her sins. She loved Jesus because He had given her brother his life back. She loved Jesus because of all He had done for her. **True worship comes from a grateful heart.**

(4) Her worship cost her dearly. The cost of the 12 ounces of expensive perfume is estimated at a year's wages for a common laborer. That would make it between $25,000 to $30,000 in today's wages. This gift was sacrificial; there were a lot of ways she could have used the

money. Probably there were some things she went without in order to give Jesus this gift. **True worship involves sacrificial giving.**

(5) Her worship blessed other worshippers. The fragrance of her gift filled the house and blessed the others who were gathered there. A person who truly worships Jesus with their life is a blessing to the church. The church is inspired and motivated by the devotion of a worshipper. People watch and learn from devoted worshippers. The whole church is blessed by devoted worship. **True worship blesses and impacts others.**

(6) She worshipped Jesus in humility. A Jewish woman's hair was her glory. Usually the only people who saw it undone would be her husband or other women. Mary worshipped Jesus in complete humility, using the most glorious part of her to wipe the basest part of her Savior: His feet. His feet – which had walked countless miles from town to town. His feet – which had brought Him to her house to heal her brother. His feet – which would be nailed to a cross in just a few days. She used the best part of herself to minister to the lowest part of Him. She sat at His feet, anointed His feet and wiped His feet. **True worship brings us humbly to the feet of Jesus,** entirely subjected to His Lordship in our lives.

(7) She was criticized and hated for her worship. People who are not fully devoted to Christ

often feel threatened by true worshippers. They feel convicted to change, and so they become critical and find things to point out to try to defile the gift. But **Jesus defends the true worshipper. Jesus commends the worship.** It is between us and Jesus. Only Jesus knows the motivation of the heart ... and Jesus knew Mary's heart was true. And so, the gift was true. And so, the worship was true.

(8) **Her worship brought glory to Jesus.** True worship glorifies God. God spent His last days where He would be glorified.

Would He spend His last days with you?

Day 60: After the Parade

John 12:12-19

Hearts That Stay True

Don't you love a good parade? It is exciting. Our town has a parade every June. The marching bands play, the baton twirlers twirl, the riding club rides their horses down Front Street, and we see decorated floats advertise all that is happening in our community. The float riders throw out candy to the kids. The mayor rides by in a convertible. Our emotions get swept up in the moment, and we cheer. Parades give us something to celebrate.

Many in the crowds lining Jerusalem's streets that day had never seen Jesus, had only heard of Him. The stories had spread of the miracles He had done, most recently raising Lazarus from the dead. People were talking, the news had spread. There were visitors from other cities and countries to celebrate the Passover in Jerusalem. Under the oppressive Roman rule, they were excited to join in the pageantry and hope of celebrating an emerging Jewish leader. And celebrate they did!

> The next day, the news that Jesus was on the way to Jerusalem swept through the city. A large crowd of Passover visitors took palm branches and went down the road to meet Him. They shouted, "Praise God! Blessings on the One Who comes in the Name of the Lord! Hail to the King of Israel!"

Jesus found a young donkey and rode on it, fulfilling the prophecy that said: "Don't be afraid, people of Jerusalem. Look, your King is coming, riding on a donkey's colt." His disciples didn't understand at the time that this was a fulfillment of prophecy. But after Jesus entered into His Glory, they remembered what had happened and realized that these things had been written about Him.

Many in the crowd had seen Jesus call Lazarus from the tomb, raising him from the dead, and they were telling others about it. That was the reason so many went out to meet Him - because they had heard about this miraculous sign.

Then the Pharisees said to each other, "There's nothing we can do. Look, everyone has gone after Him!"

John 12:12-19

How quickly hearts change! This parade was no mistake: it was planned by God, and prophesied by Zechariah hundreds of years before. Jesus knew – even as He heard the cheers of the people – how the tide would turn in a few short days. He knew this public display of favor from the crowds would seal His fate. The religious leaders would not let this go unpunished; they would react violently.

Luke tells us that Jesus wept as He approached the city:

> But as He came closer to to Jerusalem and saw the city ahead, He began to weep. "How I wish today that you of all people would understand the way to peace. But now it is too late, and peace is hidden from your eyes. Before long, your enemies will build ramparts against your walls, and encircle you and close you in from every side. They will crush you into the ground and your children with you. Your enemies will not leave a single stone in place, because you did not accept your opportunity for salvation."
>
> **Luke 19:41-44**

How quickly hearts change! As Jesus approached Jerusalem – the City of God, the people He came to save – He knew what lay ahead for them. He knew how much pain and suffering they would yet go through before truly coming to Him. He saw every war. He saw the Temple destroyed. He saw the Holocaust. And He wept.

Jesus knew how the hearts of the people would change, how the chants of praise would become taunts of rage. He saw the smiling, excited faces swept along by the emotion of the moment, and knew they would be swept away by another kind of emotion, instilled and led by the religious leaders.

But there would be those who stayed true. True hearts of worship stay true. True hearts of worship don't change when circumstances change. They don't change under pressure from others to change. True hearts of worship would, in a few short days, stand at the foot of a cross and weep. Even when the tide changes, and things are not as good as they once were, **true hearts of worship remember that God is good, and they still worship Him.**

Day 61: DNA Seeds

John 12:20-26

Testimony to God's Ancient Plan

I love watching a garden grow. I wish I could say I love weeding the garden, but honestly, I don't. I love picking out the packages of seeds I want, planting them in the ground, and waiting eagerly while they germinate under the ground. One day, they push their heads above the ground and begin their journey upward and outward. Life! Finally, fruit comes on the vine, and we get to enjoy the result of planting. What comes off the vine multiplies the seed by hundreds, perhaps even thousands of potential new seeds. What power lies in the seed! But in order for the power to be released, the seed must die and be buried.

The story of salvation is held in every seed that is buried and produces fruit. Every seed that grows into a plant and results in fruit is a testimony to the ancient plan of God. Jesus was a Seed that held the potential to produce many other seeds that would be just like Him. Eternal beings with eternal bodies. Us. But He had to die in order for His full potential to be released, and for new seeds with His DNA to come into being.

> Some Greeks who had come to Jerusalem for the Passover celebration paid a visit to Philip, who was from Bethsaida in Galilee. They said, "Sire, we want to meet Jesus." Philip told

Andrew about it, and they went together to ask Jesus.

Jesus replied, "Now the time has come for the Son of Man to enter into His glory. I tell you the truth: unless a kernel of wheat is planted in the soil and dies, it remains alone. But its death will produce many new kernels - a plentiful harvest of new lives. Those who love their life in this world will lose it. Those who care nothing for their life in this world will keep it for Eternity. Anyone who wants to be My disciple must follow Me, because My servants must be where I am. And the Father will honor anyone who serves Me."

John 12:20-26

Finding your life by losing it – this is the way of the seed. This is the way of the disciple. **Only by dying to self and being buried with Christ do we find Life, do we bear fruit.** It is the great test of God. We are placed on this Earth and we are drawn to God. When we discover Him through Christ and become a seed of His, our will begins to change.

No longer do we want to stay just a seed, protected by the hard shell of our self-will. We now have in our DNA the desire to live for Him. Christ in us gives us the longing to be planted, to no longer be committed to the aloneness of self-preservation and self-fulfillment, but to enter the soil of living for Him and living for others. We begin to die to ourselves.

It is scary, at first, giving ourselves over to the soil of dependence on Him. But as our hard shell of self-preservation cracks open, and we germinate trust in Him, we grow ... and soon our head pokes above the ground. We soon find it is so much better to live for Him and for others than to live for ourselves. It is lonely living for ourselves. We eventually die alone, still just a seed with a hard shell, never having experienced the joy of germination.

It is wonderfully fulfilling to live for Jesus, to grow in the grace and knowledge of Him, and to let our lives produce eternal fruit that only comes by dependence on Him. Fruit like: loving God ... loving others ... having the peace that comes from trusting Christ ... experiencing the joy that comes from living for something other than self, living for His glory ... becoming a faithful follower of Christ ... living in the joy of knowing He is with you, and the hope of knowing we will live with Him for Eternity. If we die now, if we follow now, if we serve now.

Knowing Jesus means dying now. Knowing Jesus means serving now, it means loving now. This is the way of the seed. This is the way of Life. God will honor tomorrow those who go the way of the seed.

Day 62: Children of the Light

John 12:27-39

My Father's Home-going

Recently, I watched my father die. It was hard, it took several months, and he was in pain from the cancer.

As he journeyed toward his last days, he detached more and more from the physical world, and attached more and more to God. As he endured humbling and uncomfortable procedures with the hospice nurses, I remember hearing his wavering voice from the bedroom, singing hymns just to get him through the discomfort.

Through it all, he was being purified in his spirit as he depended more and more on his Father to provide him with all he needed for the moment ... the same Father to Whom Jesus cried out:

> "Now My soul is deeply troubled. Should I pray, 'Father, save Me from this hour'? But this is the very reason I came! Father, bring glory to Your Name."
>
> Then a Voice spoke from Heaven, saying, "I have already brought glory to My Name, and I will do so again." When the crowd hear the Voice, some thought it was thunder, while others declared an angel had spoken to Him.
>
> **John 12:27-29**

Nobody said dying was easy, just necessary. Even Jesus, God in the flesh, struggled when it came to giving up His life. His humanity did not want to go through the pain of the cross. His deity embraced the joy of the benefit of the cross. The two equal prayers that came from His heart as He struggled: *"Father, save Me!"* and *"Father, be glorified!"*

It is troubling to die. In much smaller ways than Jesus did, we face the struggle of dying every day, perhaps many times a day:

* It may be in the choice to be loving toward your spouse when you feel unloved and alone.
* It may be in the choice to speak the truth in love to a friend, for their benefit, even though you feel afraid of the reaction.
* It may be in the choice to discipline your child, even though you are tired and it would be much easier to "let it slide."

We think it, even if we do not say it: *"Father, get me out of this! I do not want to do the 'right thing' right now."* Then the opportunity comes to identify with Jesus, as we say: *"Father, be glorified in my choice at this moment in time."* And God gives us the power to choose to glorify Him. We live out the words of Paul:

> My old self has been crucified with Christ. It is no longer I who live, but Christ lives in me. So I live in this earthly body by trusting in the Son of

> God, Who loved me and gave Himself for me.
>
> **Galatians 2:20**

Jesus clarified the "mysterious Voice" for the people:

> Then Jesus told them, "The Voice was for your benefit, not Mine. The time for judging this world has come, when Satan - the ruler of this world - will be cast out. And when I am lifted up from the Earth, I will draw everyone to Myself." He said this to indicate how He was going to die.
>
> **John 12:30-32**

What happens when we choose to die to self and let Christ be seen in our choices or actions?

(1) God brings glory to His Name – When we let Christ be seen in us, God says, *"See, that is My child. Look at the difference My son makes in his life!"* (Kurt's words)

(2) Satan gets cast out – Satan always wants us to choose the flesh, to live for ourselves. He wants us to behave badly. When we choose to live for God and others, it shrinks Satan's influence in our lives. When we resist Satan and his ways, he flees.

(3) Others are drawn to Christ – Jesus' death and resurrection draws people to God. When we die daily to self and choose to live for others, it draws them to Christ. God likes that.

> The crowd responded, "We understood from Scripture that the Messiah would live forever. How can You say the Son of Man will die? Just Who is this Son of Man, anyway?"
>
> Jesus replied, "My Light will shine for you just a little longer. Walk in the Light while you can so the darkness will not overtake you. Those who walk in the darkness cannot see where they are going. Put your trust in the Light while there is still time; then you will become children of the Light." After saying these things, Jesus went away and was hidden from them.
>
> **John 12:34-39**

When we die to self and live for God and others, it draws us into the Light. Like a seed, we germinate and press upward through the darkness of faith, toward the Light that awaits above the ground. Darkness cannot overcome us. Life becomes more and more meaningful and bright; we care less about ourselves and more about others. We can see where we are going, and it all makes sense.

Put your trust in the Light; He will draw you from the darkness of the soil into the brightness of day. Be who you are: a child of the Light.

Day 63: When People Resist God

John 12:37-50

Choose to Believe

Have you ever watched a two-year-old child when she is embarrassed or self-conscious? She covers her eyes with her hands. It is funny to watch when – in a room full of talking, laughing people – the child thinks that somehow if she can't see the people, the people can't see her. She convinces herself that despite the fact she has been in this room for the last two hours with these people, by simply covering her eyes, those people don't exist anymore. She can't see them. She chooses to believe what she wants to believe. It doesn't change the fact that there are still people in the room, it just keeps her perspective how she wants it to be.

> But despite all the miraculous signs Jesus had done, most of the people still did not believe in Him. This is exactly what Isaiah the prophet had predicted: "Lord, who has believed our message? To whom has the Lord revealed His powerful arm?"
>
> But the people couldn't believe, for as Isaiah also said: "The Lord has blinded their eyes and hardened their hearts – so that their eyes cannot see, and their hearts cannot understand, and they

cannot turn to Me and have Me heal them."

John 12:37-40

Fortunately for the two-year-old, once she removes her hands from her eyes, reality is thrust upon her and she must believe. Eventually she learns to believe what she sees.

In the Kingdom, when people resist the call of God long enough and **won't** believe, there comes a time when they **can't** believe. They have refused to see for so long that **God allows their hearts to be hardened;** only God knows when a heart is beyond the point of no return. It is a sobering thought when God gives people and nations over to their unbelief and hardness of their hearts.

We must trust the sovereignty of God in this, and remember that God knows the heart. This brings new meaning to the words of Isaiah: *"Seek ye the Lord while He may be found, call ye upon Him while He is near"* (Isaiah 55:6).

Here with the Jewish leaders, it is like God is saying: *"I gave you My best shot. If you are not going to believe what you see with your eyes – My power to heal the blind, cast out demons, make the lame walk, and raise people from the dead – then what will you believe?"* (Kurt's words)

These Jewish leaders had the benefit of even knowing the Scriptures and the opportunity to recognize prophecy being fulfilled before their eyes. In addition, they were holding back many people from coming to Jesus by the fear of excommunication from the synagogue. People were afraid to follow Jesus publicly because they thought they would lose their place of worship. So not only were these Jewish leaders refusing to believe Emmanuel – God among them – but they were also keeping people from God. They had now become God's enemy, and so Jesus allowed them to exercise their right of refusal.

> Isaiah was referring to Jesus when he said this, because he saw the future and spoke of the Messiah's glory. Many people did believe in Him, however, including some of the Jewish leaders. But they wouldn't admit it for fear that the Pharisees would expel them from the synagogue. For they loved human praise more than the praise of God.
>
> **John 12:41-43**

It is encouraging to remember that although the unbelief of the Jewish leaders was troubling, there were many people who did come to Jesus, and thousands more in the weeks after He made His journey to the cross. It is awesome to know that God never gives up on those who have the remotest possibility of coming to Him. Here we see from a practical standpoint how Jesus Himself handles the doctrine of election. Even though God knows who He has chosen and who will choose Him, He still puts it out there to the crowds and invites all to trust Him. We model Jesus. If He invites all to trust in Him, even though He is all knowing, then we should do the same. We do not know who will respond to the Holy Spirit, so we invest in every person as a potential child of God. We partner with Jesus in shouting these words:

> Jesus shouted to the crowds, "If you trust Me, you are trusting not only Me but also God Who sent Me. For when you see Me, you are seeing the One Who sent Me. I have come as a Light to shine in this dark world so that all who put their trust in Me will no longer remain in the dark.
>
> "I will not judge those who hear Me but don't obey Me for I have come to save the world and not to judge it. But all who reject Me and My message will be judged on the Day of Judgment by the truth I have spoken. I don't speak on My own authority. The Father Who sent Me has commanded Me what to say and how to say it. And I know His commands lead to Eternal Life, so I say whatever the Father tells Me to say."
>
> **John 12:44-50**

It is like Jesus is giving them His one last, best shot to believe. It is beautiful to me that even though He knows many of these people will be swept into the murderous crowd in few days, He still sees them as His sheep, His flock, who need to be shepherded even in this moment. Even though the Shepherd is about to lay His life down for His sheep, in His last moments He is still concerned about them. He is still leading them down the paths of righteousness (see Psalm 23:3). He is at that moment preparing a table for them in the presence of the enemy (see Psalm 23:5). He is showing them goodness and mercy (see Psalm 23:6) at a time when He is preparing for His own pain and death.

Oh, the beauty of our Savior. Who would want to resist a love so pure?

Day 64: The Greatest 3-Point Shot Ever

John 13:1-17

Learn to Live the Gospel

I love Basketball. I should say I *loved* Basketball when I was younger and could still play without getting hurt. For a time, it was number one in my life. I lived for the game.

I am going to date myself with this next statement, but here goes: I wish there had been a 3-point shot when I was in high school. Half of my points came from long-range shooting, and I would have scored one-third more points if there had been a 3-point shot. In 2009, they moved the 3-point line back a foot for college. Guys were just getting too good at it. Percentages dropped by one point in Men's Division 1 Basketball since they moved the line back.

Basketball is just a game. Here in John 13, Jesus shows us the greatest 3-point shot ever made. Learn how to shoot this shot, and you learn how to live the Gospel. Take your shooting stance, everyone ....

> Before the Passover Celebration, Jesus knew that His hour had come to leave this world and return to His Father. He had loved His disciples during His ministry on Earth, and now He loved them to the very end. It was time for

> supper, and the devil had already prompted Judas, son of Simon Iscariot, to betray Jesus. Jesus knew that the Father had given Him authority over everything and that He had come from God and would return to God. So He got up from the table, took off His robe, wrapped a towel around his waist, and poured water into a basin. Then He began to wash the disciples' feet, drying them with the towel He had around Him.
>
> **John 13:1-5**

Jesus' three-pointer:

(1) **Humility** – Jesus was leaving His disciples in just a few hours. He had been the glue that held them together, that kept them loving each other. He was the unity of their group, and now He was modeling it.

The leader becomes a servant to all. Washing feet was the job of a servant. Men walked around all day in the dirt with sandals on, so when it came time to relax and eat dinner, a servant would come and wash their feet. They would never think of doing that for one another.

Yet Jesus said: *"Let Me show you a new way. Do not compete with each other for position; rather prefer one another."* Jesus knew there was a competitive spirit within this group. He knew this group would blow up if they did not practice humility. Humility says: *"When your brother wins, you win."*

Rule #1 for shooting a 3-pointer: God came down from Heaven to die for sinners. Model this in your relationships. Die to your own selfishness so that others may taste of the goodness of Jesus. So that others may succeed in their walk with Jesus. It is all about Jesus.

> When Jesus came to Simon Peter, Peter said to Him, "Lord, are You going to wash my feet?"
>
> Jesus replied, "You don't understand now what I am doing, but someday you will."
>
> "No!" Peter protested. "You will never wash my feet!"
>
> Jesus replied, "Unless I wash you, you won't belong to Me."
>
> Simon Peter exclaimed, "Then wash my hands and head as well, Lord, not just my feet!"
>
> Jesus replied, "A person who has bathed all over does not need to wash, except for the feet, to be entirely clean. And you disciples are clean, but not all of you." For Jesus knew who would betray

> Him. That is what He meant when He said, "Not all of you are clean."
>
> **John 13:6-11**

(2) **Holiness** – Holiness keeps us aligned to the goal, keeps us one with Jesus. Peter resisted Jesus washing his feet, but Jesus insisted. Jesus was modeling the Gospel.

When we come to Christ and accept His provision of forgiveness for our sins, He washes us completely. He regenerates our spirits. We are born again. We are new persons in Christ. That only happens once in our life time. You only need to be born-again once. This is our Union with God through Christ.

However, as we walk through the dirty world, our feet pick up the dust of sin. Daily we need our feet washed. This happens through confessing our sin daily – even many times a day – and keeping our feet clean. This is necessary for our Communion with Christ. That is why John told us:

> If we confess our sins, He is faithful and just to forgive us our sins, and to cleanse us from all unrighteousness.
>
> **1 John 1:9**

It was pride in Peter that did not want to receive Jesus' act of humility toward him. But once Jesus told him that having dirty feet would get in the way of relationship with Him, Peter was all in. Of course, that is when Jesus told him that once you have bathed, you only need to keep your feet clean in order to stay in communion with God. So keep your feet clean. When they get dirty, when we sin, confess it immediately to stay in communion with God. I like to call it keeping the holy handy-wipes with me.

Sometimes during the day when I entertain a judgmental or prideful thought, I immediately confess it to Jesus and ask Him to wash my feet. It keeps me walking clean and in open communication and relationship with God.

> After washing their feet, He put on His robe and sat down again, and asked, "Do you understand what I was doing? You call Me 'Teacher' and 'Lord,' and you are right, because that's what I am. And since I, your Lord and Teacher, have washed your feet, you ought to wash each other's feet. I have given you an example to follow. Do as I have done to You.
>
> "I tell you the truth: slaves are not greater than their master. Nor is the messenger more important than the one who sends the message. Now that you know these things, God will bless you for doing them."

John 13:12-17

(3) **Happiness** – Practicing Humility **+** Holiness = Happiness. The ball goes in the basket, and we

score! Happiness can be defined a lot of ways; I like this definition best: *"Happiness is knowing I am doing my best to be obedient to God, and confident He is blessing me for it."*

There is nothing like the confidence of knowing we are living the way God wants us to. Obedience to God's Word brings a deep sense of well-being to my life. It brings a sense of confidence that I am in the will of God, so everything in my life will turn out the way He wants. The way He wants is always best. Remembering this always brings peace back to my life.

Peace = knowing I am in good standing with God. In my life, Peace = Happiness. Happiness comes from keeping my feet clean by confessing and repenting from sin, because I know there is nothing between me and God. I love that.

There is nothing like shooting the ball with confidence. Confidence comes from practicing and doing what Jesus told us to do.

Love with Humility. Walk in Holiness. Rest in Happiness.

(Thanks to Warren Wiersbe for the "three H's.")

Day 65: The Judas Difference

John 13:18-30

Totally Committed?

Does it bother you that someone could spend three years with Jesus and still not believe in Him? Judas Iscariot heard all the same things the other disciples heard. He saw the same miracles. He walked the same roads with Jesus. He ate meals and shared stories. But he did not believe; he never surrendered his heart to Jesus.

As we read about John's writing about Jesus' last days on Earth, he brings our attention to Judas Iscariot. Jesus said:

> "I am not saying these things to all of you; I know the ones I have chosen. But this fulfills the Scripture that says, 'The one who eats My food has turned against Me.' I tell you this beforehand so that when it happens, you will believe that I AM the Messiah. I tell you the truth: anyone who welcomes My messenger is welcoming Me, and anyone who welcomes Me is welcoming the Father Who sent Me."
>
> Now Jesus was deeply troubled, and He exclaimed, "I tell you the truth: one of you will betray Me!"

John 13:18-21

This is troubling to me. It makes me stop and wonder, *"How much am I like Judas? Do I really love Jesus? Have I really surrendered my heart to Him?"* I **think** I have ... I know I have changed over the years. But Judas never truly loved Jesus. Why? Because Judas had another love.

> The disciples looked at each other, wondering whom He could mean. The disciple Jesus loved was sitting next to Him at the table. Simon Peter motioned him to ask, "Who is He talking about?" So that disciple leaned over to Jesus and asked, "Lord, who is it?"
>
> Jesus responded, "it is the one to whom I give the bread I dip in the bowl." And when He had dipped it, He gave it to Judas, son of Simon Iscariot. When Judas had eaten the bread, Satan entered into him. Then Jesus told him, "Hurry and do what you're going to do."
>
> None of the others at the table knew what Jesus meant. Since Judas was their treasurer, some thought Jesus was telling him to go and pay for the food, or to give some money to the poor. So Judas left at once, going out into the night.
>
> **John 13:22-30**

Judas had another love. This love came between him and Jesus, like a mistress comes between a husband and a wife. The mistress gets the affection meant for the spouse. This love is what kept Judas from giving his heart to Jesus. It was the love of money. Judas loved money.

It is interesting that even though Jesus knew this about Judas, He let him take care of the finances for the group. John had already told us Judas often stole money for himself from the group:

> Not that [Judas Iscariot] cared for the poor - he was a thief, and since he was in charge of the disciples' money, he often stole some for himself.
>
> **John 12:6**

Judas loved money. Remember what Paul told Timothy about that:

> For the love of money is the root of all kinds of evil. And some people, craving money, have wandered from the true faith, and pierced themselves with many sorrows.
>
> **1 Timothy 6:10**

The troubling fact is, Judas could be around Jesus – hear Him speak powerfully, see Him heal miraculously, watch Him love extravagantly – and still not believe because his heart belonged to someone else: the powerful mistress of money. When the opportunity arose, He sold Jesus out to "his mistress" for 30 pieces of silver, which he must have thought would be worth it at the time.

Let us not miss the power of this picture. When Jesus handed Judas the bread, Judas took it and ate it ... and the deal was made. Satan himself entered into Judas through the way made available to him: another love, the love of money. Luke and Matthew wrote nearly the identical words about this:

> No one can serve two masters. For you will hate one and love the other; you will be devoted to one and despise the other. You cannot serve both God and money.
>
> **Luke 16:13** (also see **Matthew 6:24**)

Now, there are many "loves" that can get between us and Jesus, but the love of money is the one we see most. Why? Because we think money buys us security. In a word, dependence. We depend on money. Jesus wants us to depend on Him.

Our money should say: *"In this money we trust"* instead of *"In God we trust."* We do not trust God – we trust money. Why is it that people are so hesitant to obey God's word and give their first 10% back to the storehouse, the church? Because they think they need it. They depend on it. They hang on to it as though that 10% will save them. They are stealing from the group, just like Judas did.

In fact, God says they are **stealing** from Him:

> "Will a man rob God? Yet you rob Me. But you ask, 'How do we rob You?' In tithes and offerings. You are under a curse - the whole nation of you - because you are robbing Me. Bring the whole tithe into the storehouse that there may be food in My House."
>
> **Malachi 3:8-10**

The group is getting by on less because people are not tithing. God says: *"Prove to Me that you trust Me. Prove to Me that you love Me. Tithe! Show Me the money. Dependance on money is what gets between you and Me.* ***Prove to Me you trust Me, not money."*** 80% or more of people in the church in America hang around Jesus, hear His words, see His miracles, receive His forgiveness for sin, and all the benefits that come from being with Him – and yet cannot seem to trust Him with that 10%. Wow.

Are we any different than Judas?

Day 66: God In the Darkness

John 13:31-38

Darkness Flees the Light of Love

Lots of amazing things happen in the darkness. Seeds germinate ... babies grow from one cell into a complete, amazing human being ... the Son of God resurrected from a dust-body into an immortal, eternal, glorious Body. All in the dark.

> As soon as Judas left the room, Jesus said, "The time has come for the Son of Man to enter into His glory, and God will be glorified because of Him. And since God receives glory because of the Son, He will soon give glory to the Son."
>
> **John 13:31-32**

It is amazing and encouraging to me that God can use the darkest time in history to shine. Satan enters into Judas ... Judas enters into the darkness ... and Jesus enters into His Glory. It is encouraging because it reminds me that no matter how dark it seems, God is always t work for His Glory.

There is something of substance and eternity being formed in the darkness. Satan can be at work, and circumstances can look bad, but like Joseph showed us in his story: God can take the darkest, most evil situation imaginable and turn it to good. Look for God in the darkness.

> "Dear children, I will be with you only a little longer. And as I told the Jewish leaders, you will search for Me, but you can't come where I am going. So now I am giving you a new commandment: Love each other. Just as I have loved you, you should love each other. Your love for one another will prove to the world that you are My disciples."
>
> **John 13:33-35**

And while we wait in the darkness – we love. While God is at work in the darkness – we love. We love Him by obeying Him, and we love each other by serving one another. Obeying and serving – that is our job. Washing feet. Putting others' needs before our own. Being committed to sharing Christ and encouraging believers. This is what makes us different than the world, different than Judas. It makes us shine! Darkness must flee the Light of Love. People are drawn to the Light of Love.

> Simon Peter asked, "Lord, where are You going?"
>
> And Jesus replied, "You can't go with Me now, but you will follow Me later."
>
> "But why can't I come now, Lord?" he asked. "I'm ready to die for You."
>
> Jesus answered, "Die for Me. I tell you the truth, Peter: before the rooster

crows tomorrow morning, you will deny three times that you even know Me."

John 13:36-38

It was not Peter's time to die for Jesus, but one day he would: on a cross, like His Savior and Friend. For now, God had some more breaking and building to do in his life. Peter needed to reach bottom in order to really be useful in God's hand. He had to realize how limited he was in his own power to be faithful, so that God could fill him with power from on high. Peter had to come to the end of himself.

Denying Jesus three times would break Peter's heart ... and make him ready to be used mightily by God. God was at work in the darkness.

Day 67: Cure For Troubled Hearts

John 14:1-7

"Home Before You Know It"

We lived in Bothell, Washington, when our children were young. Most weekends, we would put them in our red Taurus station-wagon and make the 100-mile trip to Lynden, to see the family.

The kids hated the journey. Lindsey would promptly go to sleep to ward off motion-sickness, and Levi would occupy his time playing video games and listening to music. When they were both awake at the same time, there was plenty of whining and arguing going around. *"Dad, she's in my space"* and *"Mom, he's looking at me!"*

On the way back home, as they became more tired, I always told our kids, *"We will be home before you know it."*

> "Don't let your hearts be troubled. Trust in God, and trust also in Me. There is more than enough room in My Father's Home. If this were not so, would I have told you that I am going to prepare a place for You? When everything is ready, I will come and get you so that you will always be with Me where I am. And you know the way to where I am going?"

"No, we don't know, Lord," Thomas said. "We have no idea where You are going, so how can we know the way?"

Jesus told him, "I am the Way, the Truth and the Life. No one can come to the Father except through Me. If you had really known Me, you would know Who My Father is. From now on, you do know Him and have seen Him!"

John 14:1-7

Where do you go in your heart when you begin to get troubled with the cares and worries of this life? I go Home. I do not go home to my house or to the house where I was raised. I "go Home in my heart." I think about my real Home that Jesus has gone to prepare for me. I think about Heaven.

When we have been gone on a long trip with the kids, and they begin to get tired of traveling, and we are close to the end of our travels, what do we tell them? I always told our kids, *"We will be home before you know it."*

I sometimes get tired of this journey we are on, as good as it is. This journey can make our hearts troubled. We can get weighed down by the trouble we encounter. It helps me to know we will be Home before we know it.

When I am tempted to be troubled about investments losing money, I think about the fact that in 40 years or so, it just will not matter – ***I will***

be Home! When I am tempted to be troubled about my body getting older and things not quite working as well as they used to, I think about the fact that I am getting a brand-new body very soon.

I love to travel and explore new places, and it troubles me sometimes that I do not have the money or time to go to all the places I long to see. It helps me to realize that one day this Earth will be remade, perfectly, and we will live here and care for it. I will get to see all the places I long to see anytime I want, as long as I want (and probably no travel costs!), and the New Earth will be beautifully perfect. One day it will all be mine, and yours, through Christ. Jesus has gone before us, and because we know Jesus, our Home is with God.

Knowing we have a Home waiting for us does not make us live poorly while we are here. It does not give us a *"Who cares?"* mentality. It makes us live better, with more intention. Because we have hope, we live our lives here the best we can, influencing those around us the most we can. Because we know it will all be over soon and "we will be Home before we know it," we run hard and face trouble with the joy of knowing what awaits us. Jesus. Heaven. Home.

Take heart, my friend. Live well. Do not let your heart be troubled. You will be Home before you know it.

Day 68: In the Name of Jesus

John 14:8-14

Tremendous Responsibility

There are times when I have wished that I had lived in the days of Jesus, that I could have been one of His up-close-and-personal disciples. On the other hand, they seem like a really mixed-up bunch of people! It is easy for me to say I would have "got" Jesus all along, but when we read about "doubting Thomas" and "wishy-washy Philip," then I am not so sure I would want to be one of those men asking "silly questions"! *"Hind-sight has 20/20 vision."*

> Philip said, "Lord, show us the Father, and we will be satisfied."
>
> Jesus replied, "Have I been with you all this time, Philip, and yet you still don't know Who I am? Anyone who has seen Me has seen the Father! So why are you asking Me to show Him to you? Don't you believe that I am in the Father and the Father is in Me? The words I speak are not My own but My Father Who lives in Me does His work through Me. Just believe that I am in the Father and the Father is in Me. Or at least believe because of the work you have seen Me do."
>
> **John 14:8-11**

Here Jesus is once again reminding us that He and the Father, Almighty God, *Yahweh*, are One. Jesus Christ is God.

> "I tell you the truth: anyone who believes in Me will do the same works I have done, and even greater works, because I am going to be with the Father. You can ask for anything in My Name, and I will do it so that the Son can bring glory to the Father. Yes, ask Me for anything in My Name, and I will do it!"
>
> **John 14:12-14**

People get hung up on this Scripture and wonder why God is not giving them that new *Z-4* they asked for ... or why He did not give them an "A" on the test they did not study for. Here are a few easy guidelines for asking for *"anything"*:

(1) ***"Greater works"*** are **still** being done today. Not greater in quality than the works Jesus did, but greater in quantity and scope. Jesus is saying that when He goes to be with the Father after His resurrection, He will give them the Holy Spirit. The Holy Spirit will be poured out and be present in the lives of all believers. He will convict and convince people of their need for God like never before. Proof of this was when Peter preached the Gospel for the first time – and 3,000 people (or more) became followers of Jesus Christ on one day! It is the Holy Spirit in us that does the *"greater works."*

(2) ***"Anything in My Name"*** means we have a tremendous responsibility to know what Jesus would want. We need to know His character, His nature, and what is important to Him. We learn this from His Word. We know for sure that He loves people, and wants the lost to know Him – so we should pray for the lost to find Him. We know for sure He wants us to become deeper disciples of Him – so we should pray to be changed into His image. Praying in Jesus' Name means **praying in alignment with what pleases Him,** lines up with His Word, and brings glory to Him.

(3) **Pray in obedience.** Jesus told us how to pray, and gave us a great model for prayer: *The Lord's Prayer.* I would like to follow this model; here it is in my words. I would like to spend several minutes in each section, worshipping and praising Him, and appropriating each element over the things I am praying about.

- (a) *Father in Heaven, You are holy. I worship and praise You.*
- (b) *I pray that Your Kingdom would be established in these situations.*
- (c) *I pray that Your will would be established in these situations.*
- (d) *Thank You for giving me all I need today to meet the situations I will face.*
- (e) *Forgive me for the sin I have committed.*
- (f) *Help me in the areas of temptation I will face.*

(g) *Yours is the Kingdom, the power and the glory, forever. Praise You!*

Day 69: Obedience Is Love

John 14:15-21

Respect and Disrespect

As a father raising my children, there was one way I felt loved by them more than any other: when they did what I told them to do. On the other hand, when they were disobedient, it was then I felt the most disrespected and the least appreciated. The thought would cross my mind: *"After all I have done for you, and you cannot do this one thing?"* Hmm, I wonder if our Heavenly Dad ever feels that way?

> "If you love Me, obey My commandments. And I will ask the Father, and He will give you another Advocate Who will never leave you. He is the Holy Spirit, Who leads into all truth. The world cannot receive Him and doesn't recognize Him. But you know Him because He lives with you now and later will be in you.
>
> "No, I will not abandon you as orphans – I will come to you. Soon the world will no longer see Me, but you will see Me. Since I live, you also will live. When I am raised to life again, you will know that I am in My Father, and you are in Me and I am in you."

John 14:15-20

Jesus was preparing His disciples for the fact that He would no longer be with them physically. He would go to the cross, to the tomb, come back to life, and then go to Heaven. But He would not leave them alone: the Holy Spirit, the Spirit of Christ would come and live in each believer.

In the times before Christ came, the Holy Spirit would come and go in the lives of men and woman who walked with God. The prophets enjoyed the presence of God, and sometimes the kings did too. But now, the Holy Spirit would come and live in believers. You and I, when we received Christ, received the Holy Spirit.

He is the One Who keeps us in the truth through conviction of sin and revelation of His Word. He encourages us daily as we involve and include Him in our life. He is the One Who gives us the power to choose to not sin. When everything around us seems to be tumbling down, the Holy Spirit is the One Who keeps our lives together and our souls encouraged. He is the Comforter of any obedient child of God; we are never alone.

> "Those who accept My commandments and obey them are the ones who love Me. And because they love Me, My Father will love them. And I will love them and reveal Myself to each of them."
>
> **John 14:21**

GOD101

Do you ever wonder if you love God? We tend to think we should feel deep, meaningful feelings for God. Sometimes during church worship time, I am stirred deep within my soul with feelings of gratefulness and love for God. But not every time, and not all the time. Sometimes I wonder how well I really love God. These are feelings.

I am so thankful Jesus didn't tell us it was all about feelings – Jesus said it was about faith and obedience. All of us feel things differently, but we can each obey God. Our love for Jesus is measured by obedience, not feelings. It is similar to marriage in that love in marriage is measured – not by feelings – but by commitment. Within that commitment, we learn to treat our spouse lovingly and with respect. We learn to do things for them that they interpret as love. We say words of affirmation they need to hear.

With Jesus, we obey. In our obedience, we do loving acts for others. We open our mouths and praise Him biblically, in obedience. The Bible has a lot to say about how we can best express our praise to God. We obey by choosing to not sin, by keeping our hearts pure. We obey by bringing our finances under dependence upon Him by tithing and sharing our money with others in need.

Jesus says, *"When you obey Me, you prove your love for Me."* When we give a cup of water to someone who is thirsty, Jesus feels love. When we give a couple of hours a week teaching kids in church, we are loving Jesus.

Jesus says if we practice obedience to Him and His Word, He will reveal Himself to us even more. We get closer to Jesus, understand Him more, and live in the confidence of His presence in a more real and meaningful way.

How do we know if we love Jesus? We obey Jesus because obedience is love.

Day 70: Home, Sweet Home

John 14:22-31

Living With God

Yesterday, I watched our nation's peaceful transfer of power from one Administration to another ... and to a new President who does not hold some of the same values I believe in. Although I have concern about this new Administration and where our nation is headed, I have peace in my spirit because I know God holds the hearts of kings in His hand. **God is in control.** This will play out exactly the way God intends. I have peace in my heart because God lives there ... and where God lives, there is peace. I am so thankful God is at home in my heart.

God wants to "make His home" with us. We know that anyone who receives Christ goes to be with Him when they die – that is called salvation. God also wants to live with us – to make His home with us right now, even on this Earth – that is called submission.

When we truly turn our hearts to God and give Him our affection, He lives with us in a special way. He fellowships with us. He communes with us. We sense His presence, and we know He is near. It is a wonderful thing to be aware of God's presence in our lives. That awareness comes by daily submitting to His ways and inviting His presence into our lives. God wants to live with us, but it is up to us to invite Him in. As we allow our hearts to become more and more dependent on

Him, He builds into our lives a greater sense of His presence and a confidence that He is with us.

> Judas (not Judas Iscariot, but the other disciple with that name) said to Him, "Lord, why are You going to reveal Yourself only to us and not to the world at large?"
>
> Jesus replied, "All who love Me will do what I say. My Father will love them, and We will come and make Our home with each of them. Anyone who doesn't love Me will not obey Me. And remember: My words are not My own. What I am telling you is from the Father Who sent Me. I am telling you these things now while I am still with you. But when the Father sends the Advocate as My representative - that is, the Holy Spirit - He will teach you everything and will remind you of everything I have told you.
>
> **John 14:22-26**

I am writing this passage today in January 2009. A friend of mine lost his job this week. He had been selling for his company for 15 years. He is nearing 60 years old, a bad time to lose his job. When asked how he was doing, he answered that he is okay. He believes God has something in mind for him. He has peace because – underneath the unsettled feelings about being laid off – he knows His Father has his life in his hands.

Things did not look so good to the disciples when Jesus was arrested and on His way to the cross. I am sure they were unsettled in their hearts. But God never lost control – He had a plan and worked it to His glory. He will do it again; this brings me peace.

> "I am leaving you with a gift: peace of mind and heart. And the peace I give as a gift, the world cannot give. So don't be troubled or afraid. Remember what I told you: I am going away, but I will come back to you again. If you really loved Me, you would be happy that I am going to the Father, Who is greater than I am. I have told you these things before they happen so that when they do happen, you will believe."
>
> **John 14:27-29**

Obedient love and commitment embraces the bigger picture. God is up to more than our personal comfort. As He was talking about peace, Jesus was preparing to submit His life to the working of His enemy, Satan. He was committed to the big picture. He knew there would be pain, darkness and separation from His Father, but He knew it was temporary and necessary. He was committed to the outcome, the big picture: glorious eternal life for His own children.

True love and commitment to Christ looks past the temporary, painful circumstances of this world into the eternal, glorious purposes of God. Peace of mind and heart comes when we focus more on the glorious finish and less on the painful process.

> "I don't have much more time to talk to you because the ruler of this world approaches. He has no power over Me, but I will do what the Father requires of Me so that the world will know that I love the Father.
>
> "Come, let's be going."

John 14:30-31

Obedient love says, *"Come, let's be going."* The best is yet to come!

Day 71: Prune, Cut, Graft

John 15:1-11

The Vine and the Branches

If grape-branches could talk, would they say they liked being pruned? Would they say it is uncomfortable, even painful at times? Yes ... but would they say they are thankful for the caring gardener who keeps them producing the best fruit? Would they say they are thankful for how he prunes away dead wood that harbors deadly pests and rot? Yes, because the gardener cares about his plants.

> "I am the true Grapevine and My Father is the Gardener. He cuts off every branch of Mine that doesn't produce fruit, and He prunes the branches that do bear fruit so they will produce even more.
>
> "You have already been pruned and purified by the message I have given you. Remain in Me, and I will remain in you. For a branch cannot produce fruit if it is severed from the Vine, and you cannot be fruitful unless you remain in Me."
>
> **John 15:1-4**

A loving, caring gardener cares for his plants by pruning them. In fact, he is not loving them when he lets them grow wild and produce inferior fruit or even no fruit. A plant that produces no fruit is pulled out and burned.

The most unloving God could be to us is leave us alone and not prune us. He is closest to us when He is pruning. He pays close attention and makes every cut just right. He cuts away dead wood – old sinful patterns and ways of thinking that hurt us. What is the dead wood in your life? He also cuts away living tissue – ways of living or useless activity that robs us of our vitality and productivity. We call those branches "suckers." Suckers take a lot of energy in our life, and produce no fruit. What are the suckers in your life?

God prunes us so that we produce the best fruit. What kind of fruit is God looking for in our life? Warren Wiersbe gives us some examples of fruit:

(1) *We bear fruit when we win others to Christ* (see Romans 1:13)
(2) *We are a part of the harvest* (see John 4:35-38)
(3) *As we grow in holiness and obedience, we are bearing fruit* (see Romans 6:22)
(4) *Paul considered Christian giving to be fruit from a dedicated life* (see Romans 15:28)
(5) *The fruit of the Spirit* (see Galatians 5:22-23) *is the kind of Christian character that glorifies God and makes Christ real to others*
(6) *Our good works, our service, grow out of our abiding life* (see Colossians 1:10)

(7) *Praise that comes from our hearts and lips is actually fruit to the glory of God* (see Hebrews 13:15).

How do we best produce the best fruit? We stay strongly attached to the Vine. For a grape-branch, it is natural to stay attached to the vine. For us, it takes humility, intention, submission and self-sacrifice to "remain" in the Vine, Jesus Christ:

> "Yes, I am the Vine; you are the branches. Those who remain in Me and I in them will produce much fruit. For apart from Me, you can do nothing. Anyone who does not remain in Me is thrown away like a useless branch, and withers. Such branches are gathered into a pile to be burned. But if you remain in Me and My words remain in you, you may ask for anything you want, and it will be granted! When you produce much fruit, you are My true disciples. This brings great glory to My Father.
>
> "I have loved you even as the Father has loved Me. Remain in My love. When you obey My commandments, you remain in My love, just as I obey My Father's commandments and remain in His love. I have told you these things so that you will be filled with My joy. Yes, your joy will overflow!"

John 15:5-11

Once we receive Christ, we are grafted into the Vine and become branches. The proof that we are truly branches – or disciples of Him – is that we produce more and more fruit. And the fruit becomes better and better fruit. Again, what is this fruit? Review the seven examples above. Are we producing these fruits more and more as God prunes in our lives? Are we open to Him pruning in our lives? Do we see areas of our lives that need to be pruned?

Remember: God loves us enough to give us the special, necessary attention of pruning. Humility – the ability to see ourselves as God sees us – is the key to opening ourselves up to His perfect pruning. Embrace the fact that we all need pruning.

As we say goodbye to our old identities – our old ways of thinking, old patterns of behaving – we then say hello to our new identities in Christ – new ways of thinking and new patterns of behaving that produce loads and loads of beautiful, wonderful fruit and bring Glory to God, our loving Gardener!

Day 72: *"Give-Give"*

John 15:9-17

True Friendship

Have you ever been in a one-sided friendship? You know the kind: where you feel like you are the one doing all of the giving, and your "friend" is just taking? That is really not friendship at all. Friendship is a "give-give" relationship, where there is no taking, but we each benefit from what the other gives. Jesus said:

> "I have loved you even as the Father has loved Me. Remain in My love. When you obey My commandments, you remain in My love, just as I obey My Father's commandments and remain in His love. I have told you these things so that you will be filled with My joy. Yes, your joy will overflow!
>
> "This is My commandment: Love each other in the same way I have loved you. There is no greater love than to lay down one's life for one's friends. You are My friends if you do what I command."
>
> **John 15:9-14**

Jesus is our Friend. He proved His friendship by how He gave. He was so committed to us that He gave up His glorious position in Heaven; then during His life here on Earth, He traded comfort for pain ... and even His fellowship with His Father was broken for that one and only time to win our friendship. Jesus chose to be our Friend. He chose to be your Friend.

Friendship is give-give. Jesus did His part to be our Friend: He chose to give His life for us. What do we choose to give to make the friendship a true, authentic, "give-give" relationship? We give love. Jesus gave us unconditional, sacrificial love, which in turn gives us the ability to love Him and love others. The friendship is complete when we choose to love God with our whole heart, and choose to be loving toward people. This is not compulsion – it is friendship.

> "I no longer call you slaves, because a master doesn't confide in his slaves. Now you are My friends, since I have told you everything the Father told Me. You didn't choose Me - I chose you. I appointed you to go and produce lasting fruit, so that the Father will give you whatever you ask for, using My Name. This is My command: Love each other."
>
> **John 15:15-17**

Being friends with a King is a little different than any other friendship! The King still has His position to uphold and His authority to use. He does not stop being King just because He is our Friend – He is still our King.

You and I are friends of the King. To be friends of the King means we are in His inner circle. We have access to His knowledge, His ideas, His plans and His heart. He shares His life with us. We are drawn even closer into friendship because of the way the King trusts us with His thoughts and His plans. The King chooses to reveal His heart to us, His friends.

How do we respond to that trust? We become loyal to the King. We buy in. We agree with the plan. We choose to participate fully and help carry out the plan, because He chose to "bring us in on it."

That reminds me of *"The Lord of the Rings,"* of the nine friends who pledged their lives to complete the quest to save all of Mankind from evil. Once they were "all in," they fought to the death to fulfill the mandate, producing great fruit and saving many from evil. The friendship became true because of the "give-give." Each one gave what they could give, fully and completely, to the death.

Jesus gave, so we give. That is friendship. Be loyal to the King. Love God, Love People.

Day 73: So You Had a Bad Day

John 15:18-27

Expect Persecution

Did you ever get the feeling someone does not like you, and you do not know why? You think, *"What did I do to make them hate me?"* Well, maybe it is not you they hate – perhaps they hate Christ in you.

> "If the world hates you, remember that it hated Me first. The world would love you as one of its own if you belonged to it, but you are no longer part of the world. I chose you to come out of the world, so it hates you. Do you remember what I told you: 'A slave is not greater than the master'? Since they persecuted Me, naturally they will persecute you. And if they had listened to Me, they would listen to you.
>
> "They will do all this to you because of Me, for they have rejected the One Who sent Me. They would not be guilty if I had not come and spoken to them. But now they have no excuse for their sin. Anyone who hates Me also hates the Father. If I hadn't done such miraculous signs among them that no one else could do, they would not be guilty. But as it is, they have seen everything I did, yet

> they still hate Me and My Father. This fulfills what is written in their Scriptures: 'They hated me without cause.'"

John 15:18-25

There is a spiritual world we cannot see or feel physically. There are spiritual forces in opposition to the Spirit of Christ Who lives in us. Should it surprise us that sometimes we sense that resistance, that opposition, from certain people? Should it surprise us that sometimes even our circumstances might reflect that "the world" and its social and political systems in opposition to Jesus Christ, Who lives in us?

There will be times we do not have favor with "the world" because we are identified with Christ. At those times, it is important to remember that we do not wrestle against people, but against spiritual forces. We are still called to be loving toward people because, honestly, they may not even realize why they are in opposition against us. It is their spiritual influence, Satan, in opposition against Christ in us.

Maybe it is a business contract we do not get ... maybe it is a position we do not win ... maybe it is not getting the playing time we have earned on the sports field or court. Remember: the world hates Christ; so, by association, the world hates you.

Warren Wiersbe says: *"The world system functions on the basis of conformity. As long as a person follows the fads and fashions and accepts the values of the world, he or she will 'get along.' But the Christian refuses to be* 'conformed to this world' *and so may be rejected by this world. Often people don't even realize they are in opposition to you. Because they belong to the world, they let the spirit of the world work through them, often without their realization, and always without cause. But even so, because they have rejected Christ, they will be held accountable in the end for their sin."*

Is it wonderful that God did not leave us alone to struggle with this opposition? Yes! Read on ...

> "But I will send you the Advocate – the Spirit of truth. He will come to you from the Father and will testify all about Me. And you must also testify about Me because you have been with Me from the beginning of My ministry."
>
> **John 15:26-27**

Expect persecution – it is happening all over the world. Christian people are being tortured and put to death for their faith in Christ, as I write this. It is a normal part of identifying with Christ. That is why it is so awesome we have the Holy Spirit living in us, to encourage us. He comforts us any time we are opposed. He gives us the power to stand up for Jesus at all times. He feeds our soul with Truth from the Word of God as we read it daily. The Holy Spirit is our friend, our Advocate, the One Who stands beside us as we face opposition of every kind.

The next time you think there is opposition from someone who is not a believer, ask the question: *"Is this a spiritual battle?"* When you do, remember it is still our goal to love the person who opposes us, because they too are made in the image of God. They are the *"whosoever"* Jesus died for on the cross. Rather than oppose – yield, pray, love, and share. That is what to do *"when people hate you."*

Day 74: The World

John 16:1-4

On Love and Hate

"If the world hates you, remember that it hated Me first."

John 15:18

What is "the world"? When we listen to the radio news, we may hear the announcer say: *"And now the news from the world of Sports!"* Obviously, "the world of Sports" is not a special country or a planet where everybody lives who is connected in some way with Sports. "The world of Sports" refers to all the organizations, people, plans, activities, philosophies, etc., that are a part of Sports. Some of these things are visible and some are invisible, but all of them are organized around one thing: Sports.

"The world" from a Christian point-of-view involves all the people, plans, organizations, activities, philosophies, values, etc. that belong to society **without God.** Some of these may be very cultural, others may be very corrupt, but all of them have their origins in the heart and mind of sinful man and promote what sinful man wants to enjoy and accomplish. As Christians, we must be careful not to love the world (see 1 John 2:15-17) or be conformed to the world (see Romans 12:1-2).

Jesus pulls no punches when He tells His disciples that their situation in the world will be serious and even dangerous. Note the progress in the world's opposition: hatred (see John 15:18-19) ... persecution (see John 15:20) ... excommunication, and even death (see John 16:2). We can trace these stages of resistance as we read the Books of Acts. Jesus goes on to warn His disciples:

> "I have told you these things so that you won't abandon your faith. For you will be expelled from the synagogues, and the time is coming when those who kill you will think they are doing a holy service for God. This is because they have never known the Father or Me. Yes, I'm telling you these things now so that when they happen, you will remember My warning. I didn't tell you earlier because I was going to be with you for a while longer."
>
> **John 16:1-4**

For Jesus' disciples, the persecution would be immediate and intense. Their lives would be at risk for the rest of their lives. It is interesting to me that one of the persecutors whom Jesus was writing about was Saul – who would encounter Jesus on the road to Damascus and become the greatest writer of the New Testament. His name would become Paul, and he would take the Gospel to the Gentiles and establish churches in key places around the known world. He too would eventually suffer persecution and die in prison.

Here in the West, we do not (yet) experience the level of persecution Jesus is warning His disciples about. However, I believe a time is coming when the Church of Christ will be more clearly defined by commitment to Biblical morals and following Christ. We will be defined by standing for the unborn ... by staying true to Biblical marriage and relationships ... by loving the sinner but not the sin. Remember: Jesus said that through it all, *"The world will know you are my followers by your love for one another."* Persecution will highlight our love better.

Day 75: Changing Places

John 16:5-15

An Exchange

Have you ever had a best friend leave you? Someone you were really close to, and they were an important part of your life? Is it hard to be happy for him (or her) because of the loss you feel? When my son left for college, it was really hard because I miss him. When my daughter moved to Scotland to work with *Youth With A Mission,* I cried when I went into her empty, quiet room. At the same time, I was very excited and happy for them for the growth and changes that God was orchestrating in their lives. It is the right thing.

It seems like the disciples were only concerned about their immediate loss of Jesus leaving them, and not the big picture of what this would mean for the Church. Jesus called them on it:

> "But now I am going away to the One Who sent Me, and not one of you is asking where I am going. Instead, you grieve because of what I've told you. But in fact, it is best for you that I go away, because if I don't, the Advocate (Comforter, Encourager, Counselor) won't come. If I do go away, then I will send Him to you."
>
> **John 16:5-7**

Jesus was going back to His Father. His physical presence on Earth was coming to an end. But in exchange, the Holy Spirit would come and make His home in the hearts of people, those who received Christ. Instead of God living in one man, Jesus, God would now live in **everyone who believed.** That is a great exchange. However, all the disciples could think about was losing their Friend and Leader Jesus. Can you blame them? They did not know what was going on. It is easier for us; we get to read about it.

> "And when He comes, He will convict the world of its sin, and of God's righteousness, and of the coming judgment. The world's sin is that it refuses to believe in Me. Righteousness is available because I go to the Father, and you will see Me no more. Judgment will come because the ruler of this world has already been judged."
>
> **John 16:8-11**

The Holy Spirit does so much for us:

(1) **Holy Spirit convicts the world of sin, the sin of unbelief:** It is the sin of unbelief in Christ that condemns a sinner to Hell. The Holy Spirit – through the faithful witness of believers and the truth of His Word – exposes the unbelief of the world.

(2) **Holy Spirit convicts the world of the righteousness of Jesus Christ:** When Jesus walked the Earth, He was accused of

blasphemy, of breaking the Law deceiving, and even having demons. The Holy Spirit convicts the world of the righteousness of Christ by how we let Him shine through us, and by the truth in God's Word.

(3) **Holy Spirit convicts the lost sinner of judgment:** that judgment Jesus made over Satan and evil when He conquered death and the grave. The Holy Spirit helps the unbeliever see the hopelessness of belonging to the world and living for self.

Jesus goes on to say:

"There is so much more I want to tell you, but you can't bear it now. When the Spirit of Truth comes, He will guide you into all truth. He will not speak on His own but will tell you what He has heard. He will tell you about the future. He will bring Me glory by telling you whatever He receives from Me. All that belongs to the Father is Mine; this is why I said, 'The Spirit will tell you whatever He receives from Me.'"

John 16:12-15

What else do we need to know about the Holy Spirit?

(4) **Holy Spirit is our Guide.** He reveals truth to us as we read the Word of God, and brings change to our lives, our patterns of living and relating through receiving of this truth.

(5) **Holy Spirit has told us about the future through the Word of God.** All we need to know about the future for life and hope is in the Word.
(6) **Holy Spirit always speaks on behalf of the Godhead: the Father and the Son.** He is in full agreement with the Word at all times. He will only speak what lines up with the Truth of God's Word.
(7) **Holy Spirit's leading in our lives will always agree with the commands of Christ,** summed up in the Great Commandment: *"Love God with all your heart, and love your neighbor as yourself."*

The more we get to know the Holy Spirit, the more we get to know Jesus. They are the One and same God. It is the Spirit Who lives in us and speaks to us all day long. You see, God never really went away: He just changed places.

Day 76: Recycling Pain

John 16:16-22

When Tragedy Meets Grace

"Jeff" has lived through a lot of truly painful things. When he was a young boy, he was sexually abused by an older neighbor boy. As an adult, intimacy was difficult for him ... and because his wife did not understand his brokenness, she could not deal with a man who couldn't connect; she abandoned him.

Jeff turned to alcohol to numb the pain, and eventually lost his job because he simply could not keep his commitments. When he finally hit bottom, he reached out to God for His love, acceptance and forgiveness. Fractured, and in a life of wreckage and ruin, he could not see how God could possibly use any of his pain for good.

Now, years later, God is using him to help others. God is redeeming the pain. In fact, the pain now seems like a distant memory. Yes, he can still remember the pain of what he had been through, but now – because of God's faithful healing of his emotions, and being used to help others facing the same kinds of struggles – there is a deep sense of joy in his life. A sense of significance that God is really using him to make a difference in the lives of others.

Jesus encouraged His disciples with these words:

"In a little while you won't see Me anymore. But in a little while after that, you will see Me again."

Some of the disciples asked each other, "What does He mean when He says, 'In a little while you won't see Me again, but then you will see Me' and 'I am going to the Father'? And what does He mean by 'a little while'? We don't understand."

Jesus realized they wanted to ask Him about it, so He said "Are you asking yourselves what I meant? I said in 'a little while you won't see Me, but a little while after that you will see Me again.' I tell you the truth: you will weep and mourn over what is going to happen to Me, but the world will rejoice. You will grieve, but your grief will suddenly turn to wonderful joy.

"It will be like a woman suffering the pains of labor. When her child is born, her anguish gives way to joy because she has brought a new baby into the world. So you have sorrow now, but I will see you again; then you will rejoice, and no one can rob you of that joy."

John 16:16-22

God is amazing at recycling pain! He has done it in my life, and He will do it in yours if you will let Him. *"What do you mean, Kurt?"* Well, this world is full of trouble and pain because of sin. We all face trouble and pain in this life, we each grieve over the things that happen to us. God is present with us to walk with us through those times. His desire is for us to become dependent on Him through it all, to hope in Him alone and to put our trust in Him alone. Ultimately, He wants to use our story – when our tragedy met His grace – to bring hope to those who are struggling. He wants our story to glorify God with this statement: *"No matter what I face, God is good. No matter what I go through, He is enough for me."*

The Bible is filled with stories of people who walked this very road in their life with Jesus. In fact, I would say it is the norm for the Christian to be drawn to God and learn about His mercy by facing and negotiating hard times in life. How would we ever learn about God's love and grace if we never have occasion to need it?

Are you facing difficulties? Have you had pain in the past? Let God take you through a healing process so that in the end, your grief turns to the joy of knowing He was always with you ... He never abandoned you ... He grieves with you ... and He wants to rejoice with you. No matter what happens in life, believe God is good, and He is enough. No one can take that away.

Day 77: Between the Cross and the Stone

John 16:23-33

We Are Never Alone

Frequently, when some woman is sharing her story with me, she tells about a time in her childhood when she was significantly hurt. Almost always the question comes up: *"Where was God when this happened to me? Why did not He stop it from happening?"*

There are no easy answers to this question. There is only **trust**. This question always brings me back to the mystery of not understanding God and His ways ... His purposes for us in this short time on Earth ... and His perfect understanding of who we each are and what we can endure. This question always brings my faith back to one choice: trust. Trust simply chooses, *"This I know: God is good, and He is enough. God is Good, and He is enough!"*

> "At that time you won't need to ask Me for anything. I tell you the truth: you will ask the Father directly, and He will grant your request because you use My Name. You haven't done this before. Ask - using My Name - and you will receive, and you will have abundant joy."
>
> **John 16:23-24**

What does it mean to use the Name of Jesus? It means we are asking something He would agree with, something that would bring God glory, something in His will. That is why – when we really do not know God's will – the best way to pray is like Jesus prayed: *"Father, Your will be done."*

As I grow closer to God, I pray these words more and more. I am finding I cannot presume what God is up to in a person's life, because I don't know the heart of every person. God does ... so I like to agree with Him! Ask in Jesus' Name, ask for God's best ... but remember that ultimately our requests *should* bring glory to God. If it brings glory to God, it will bring us joy. We can presuppose that God's will always includes a lost soul being saved, and a saved soul being transformed in character. These two things are always in the will of God, and something Jesus would agree with.

> "I have spoken these matters in figures of speech, but soon I will stop speaking figuratively and will tell you plainly about the Father. Then you will ask in My Name. I'm not saying I will ask the Father on your behalf, for the Father Himself loves you dearly because you love Me and believe that I came from God. Yes, I came from the Father into the world, and now I will leave the world and return to the Father."

John 16:25-28

Jesus is saying we can come to God directly with our needs, with assurance that He loves us and wants His best for us. His best always revolves around eternal qualities like salvation, trust in Him and character change. .

> Then His disciples said, "At last You are speaking plainly and not figuratively. Now we understand that You know everything and there's no need to question You. From this we believe that You came from God."
>
> Jesus asked, "Do you finally believe? But the time is coming – indeed, it's here now – when you will be scattered, each one going his own way, leaving Me alone. Yet, I am not alone because the Father is with Me."
>
> **John 16:29-31**

Jesus said, *"Yet I am not alone."* We are not alone. Even though we feel alone, even though everyone else abandons us, we are not alone. Even Jesus had to embrace this with faith.

"Where is God when I hurt?" **He is with us.** *"Well then, what is God doing when I hurt?"* **He is hurting with us, grieving with us, present with us, here to comfort.** God is here to weave His story with our story. You see, there is something greater than pain: it is the redemption of pain.

Redemption of pain is God's story. It is pain that makes God's story even more glorious. It is God's faithfulness and healing from pain that highlights the amazing nature of redemption, the buying-back of damaged and broken people, ruin and wreckage. He did it with Jesus for our benefit; He does it with us for His glory. Jesus partnered with God in pain; so may we.

Jesus said, *"I am not alone"* – but actually, there would be a time when He was alone: the time between the cross and the stone. Jesus would be alone, separated from the Father and the Spirit during His darkest time. He would take on the sin of the world – my sin, your sin – alone. He would endure the greatest pain, unimaginable to us, for the sake of the glory of God. He would do it in utter and total separation. Why? So that we would never have to face pain and abuse alone. God could have abandoned us, but Jesus took our abandonment upon Himself so that we would never have to suffer alone.

This is God's story, for the redemption of pain, for the glory of God. This is our story, for pain invites us to God.

Why does God allow us to experience pain? Because there is something greater than pain: **there is joy on the other side of the stone.** There is the joy of knowing the restoring power of God in my life. There is the joy of becoming dependent on Him like never before. There is joy of embracing blind trust that says, "God, I don't understand, but this I know: You are good, and You are enough."

Faith is blind – it is meant to be. We believe in what we cannot see, in what we do not fully understand. Why? Because of the glorious life that awaits us.

Peter – who himself died in the excruciating pain of crucifixion – reminded us:

> All praise to God, the Father of our Lord Jesus Christ. It is by His great mercy that we have been born again, because God raised Jesus Christ from the dead. Now we live with great expectation, and we have a priceless inheritance - an inheritance that is kept in Heaven for you, pure and undefiled, beyond the reach of change and decay. And through your faith, God is protecting you by His power until you receive this salvation, which is ready to be revealed on the Last Day for all to see. So be truly glad.
>
> There is wonderful joy ahead, even though you have to endure many trials for a little while. These trials will show that your faith is genuine. It is being tested as fire tests and purifies gold - though your faith is far more precious than mere gold. So when your faith remains strong through many trials, it will bring you much praise and glory

> and honor on the Day when Jesus Christ is revealed to the whole world. You love Him even though you have never seen Him. Though you do not see Him now, you trust Him; and you rejoice with a glorious, inexpressible joy. The reward for trusting Him will be the salvation of your souls.
>
> **1 Peter 1:3-9**

God is committed to preserving and perfecting our souls, not our bodies. It is our immortal souls that He died for. Our bodies are temporary and – in light of Eternity – quite insignificant. It is difficult for us to grasp that because for now we are mortal human with human bodies, and pain has a way of making us focus on our bodies and the emotions that are impacted by abuse. But God is committed to preserving and restoring your soul when it has been touched by abuse and pain.

When I am in pain, my world is all about me. God desires to work that out of us, wants us to remember Him and remember others in our pain. When Jesus was in pain – great physical and emotional pain – it was all about us and all about the Father. We are not alone in our pain. Many have gone before us and walked the path of restoration with Jesus. Some – like the writer of this book, John – have even died in their pain. Millions of unborn babies have tried to tell us about their pain with silent screams. We do not hear them, but even they are not alone. He is with them.

The story of pain is the story of redemption. It is truly the journey between the cross and the stone. It is the story of God overcoming the world. It is the realization that there is not bigger and better awaiting us, but BIGGEST and BEST. If we could glimpse just for a second what awaits us in the Real World, God's World, our momentary pain, our abuse – as hard as it is – would immediately take on smaller dimensions. This need not minimize our pain, but maximize our hope in His glory. One day we will see. One day we will know. One day it will all make sense. Until then we trust: God is Good. He is enough. Jesus said

> "I have told you all this so that you may have peace in Me. Here on Earth you will have many trials and sorrows. But take heart, because I have overcome the world."

John 16:33

Day 78: Glory!

John 17:1-5

The Key to a Worthwhile Life

What are you good at? When I was young, it was Basketball for me. I loved the game, I lived the game. I discovered I could feel valued and accepted by getting good at the game and by winning games. There was glory in the game. I loved the glory!

> After saying all these things, Jesus looked up to Heaven and said, "Father, the hour has come. Glorify Your Son so He can give glory back to You. For You have given Him authority over everyone. He gives Eternal Life to each one You have given Him.
>
> "And this is the way to have Eternal Life: to know You, the only true God, and Jesus Christ, the One You sent to Earth. I brought glory to You here on Earth by completing the work You gave Me to do. Now, Father, bring Me into the glory We shared before the world began."
>
> **John 17:1-5**

We do not think about God's Glory every day ... but we should. Glory is the key to living a life that is worthy of following Christ. What do I mean?

For most of us, Life is about us. It is about our families. It is about making a living. It is about being successful. It is about watching our favorite TV shows or enjoying our hobbies, at the end of the day. It is about negotiating the pains and disappointments in Life.

God's Glory changes the focus of our lives. It changes how we respond in every situation. Glory makes Life not about us, but about God. Either we live Life for ourselves, or we live it for God.

God's Glory changes how we process pain. It changes how we embrace success. Life itself is the transition from self-centered existence to living for God's Glory. Jesus needed no transition: He came ready to step into His role as a Glory-Giver. He lived His entire life for the Glory of the Father, glory that He would one day share.

We can too. More and more, day by day, we can choose to live for God's Glory.

How do we respond when we have been hurt? Does disappointment harden our hearts or drive us to the understanding lap of our Heavenly Father? Does the state of our economy make us fearful, or more dependent on the provision of our Father? Is Life about us, or about sharing the love of God?

We were born selfish; we are each in transition to living more for His glory. May you live gloriously today.

Day 79: His From the Start

John 17:6-12

Passing On Our Faith

Whom has God given to you? God gives each of us people to pass on our faith. He gives us parents ... and we have the joy of passing our faith on to them by honoring them the best we can. We have friends ... and we pass on our faith by being a good influence on them, speaking the truth to them in love, and loving them sacrificially. If you are married, you have a spouse ... to whom you pass your faith on by being faithful, loving sacrificially and living with respectfully. If you have children ... you pass on your faith by raising them in God's ways, loving them even while disciplining them and teaching them God's Word. God has given each of us someone to whom we pass on our faith.

In His heartfelt prayer with His Heavenly Father, Jesus discussed His twelve disciples ...

> "I have revealed You to the ones You gave Me from this world. They were always Yours. You gave them to Me, and they have kept Your word. Now they know that everything I have is a gift from You for I have passed on to them the message You gave Me. They accepted it and know that I came from You, and they believe You sent Me."
>
> **John 17:6-8**

The poet Shakespeare wrote: *"What's in a name?"* (*"Romeo and Juliet,"* Act II, scene 2). In the Old Testament, children were given their names for a specific purpose. Isaac was named *"laughter"* because his mother laughed when she was told she was going to have a baby in her old age. ***Immanuel*** – which is what the angel called Jesus – means *"God with us."*

God has a Name; in fact, several names that describe Him to people. Some of His Names translated include "Healer" (*Rapha*) ... "Provider" (*Jireh*) ... and "Present with us" (*Shammah*). When Jesus says, *"I have manifested Thy Name"* (verse 11; KJV), He is saying, *"I have revealed the nature of God"* or *"I have shown you God's character."*

Jesus makes it clear that His disciples had belonged to the Father before they were given to Him. It was His job to give them back to the Father, men who now understood the character of His Father, their Father. Jesus passed on His faith by living out the character of God before them.

> "My prayer is not for the world but for those You have given Me because they belong to You. All who are Mine belong to You, and You have given them to Me, so they bring Me glory. Now I am departing from the world; they are staying in this world, but I am coming to You. Holy Father, You have given Me Your Name; now protect them by the power of

Your Name so that they will be united just as we are."

John 17:9-11

Whom has God given to you? If He has given them to you, then they were His to begin with. All we are to do is live out the character of God before them. We do this well if we know our Father well.

What is God's character? Paul tells us in Galatians 5 that we reveal God when we live in love, joy, peace, patience, kindness, goodness, faithfulness, gentleness, and self-control. So we live out God's character before those whom God gives to us, and we teach them as Jesus did to let them know it is Christ in us Who enables us to be loving, good and faithful. If we try to teach them without living out the character of God, they do not get it. It does not make sense. It does not add up. For the Bible to make sense to those God has given us, the words you say must match the way you live and speak.

There is one more thing Jesus said which it is so important to remember:

"During My time here, I protected them by the power of the Name You gave Me. I guarded them so that not one was lost, except the one headed for destruction, as the Scriptures foretold.:

John 17:12

How do we protect those God gave us? The same way Jesus did: we pray for them faithfully. Every day. Many times through the day. Release them into the loving care of our Heavenly Father. Remember: they were His before they were ours. He loves them even more than we could ever possibly imagine. I know it is painful, but we must remember that He will be faithful to them. If they are His, then they are His.

Also remember that Jesus only gave back to God those God had given Him. There was one man, Judas, who was close to Jesus. He was in his life daily. For those looking on, they would have assumed Judas was one of His. But Judas had never belonged to God. So He never belonged to Jesus. Even though Jesus revealed God's character to Judas as well as the rest of the disciples, the outcome was in God's hands. God is good, God knows the heart of every person. We must trust this is true.

Who has God given you? Live out the character of God, with God's help, before them. Speak the truth to them in love when you have opportunity. Pray daily for them. And give them back to God every day. After all, they are His to begin with.

Day 80: The Fabric of Heaven

John 17:13-19

Belonging!

I love to belong, to be included. I have always desired to belong, to be accepted, to be included, to be invited. I love belonging to a team, a group, a study, my church. Have you ever heard your friends are having a party and you were not invited? Did it feel like you were left out? Did you feel a little sad because it felt, if only briefly, that you did not belong?

We long to belong. Part of the endless, hopeless searching in this world is the search to belong. You see, we each have woven deep into our soul the fabric of Heaven. We know innately we belong somewhere, and Life is a search for that belonging. We try to satisfy the longing for belonging by belonging to something, anything. Even on *Facebook,* you can belong to little cyber-clubs like: *"I bet I can find 1,000,000 Christians on Facebook"* group, or even belong to the prestigious group that is committed to watching *"Lost."* Anything to belong.

Jesus designed us to belong, and gave us what we were meant to belong to. Jesus prayed to His Father:

> "Now I am coming to You. I told them many things while I was with them in this world so they would be filled with My joy. I have given them Your Word.

> And the world hates them because they do not belong to the world, just as I do not belong to the world. I'm not asking You to take them out of the world but to keep them safe from the evil one. They do not belong to this world any more than I do.
>
> "Make them holy by Your Truth; teach them Your Word, which is Truth. Just as You sent Me into the world, I am sending them into the world. And I give Myself as a Holy Sacrifice for them so they can be made holy by Your Truth."
>
> **John 17:13-19**

Belonging makes us feel good. Belonging to Jesus is even better. It fills us with a deep sense of joy from being accepted by God, having our identity in Him, not having to work so hard to belong to the world, and knowing we have the Truth. It is hard work to have to belong to the world. The world has a great many expectations on us if we want to belong. But to belong to God – we just let Him love us. Let His love fill us. Let His love change us. **Belong to His love.**

Belonging to God gives us:

(1) **Joy** – knowing we have eternal significance
(2) A deep sense of **acceptance**, by our Creator
(3) **Protection** from evil – Satan cannot touch our souls

(4) **Holiness** through Christ's sacrifice – set aside for God
(5) A great **purpose** – being sent into the world
(6) Possessing the **Truth** – everyone wants to know the truth
(7) **Family** – the Church is our true brothers and sisters
(8) **Hope** – our pain and disappointment is temporary; we belong to God Eternally.

Whenever you feel that longing for belonging, remember: you belong!

Day 81: We Are One

John 17:20-21

Oneness Drives Desire

I used to love to play with mercury. No, mercury was not the name of my dog – mercury, the mineral, as in what comes out of a thermometer. When I was a kid, every now and then the family thermometer would mysteriously "break," and then Mom would let us play with the mercury. (Never mind that you can die from mercury poisoning; we did not know that back then.)

The cool thing about mercury is that you put it in a cup and you could get it to go into separate little balls that would roll around, like beads of liquid silver. But if they so much as touched each other, they melted into one big ball as though they had never been separate. It was like they were being drawn back into one, that they were meant to be one. We are created to be one.

> "I am praying not only for these disciples but also for all who will ever believe in Me through their message. I pray that they will all be One, just as You and I are One - as You are in Me, Father, and I am in You. And may they be in us Us so that the world will believe You sent Me."

John 17:20-21

Ponder this: our spirits came from God. I believe the eternal part of us came from Him, is one with Him, and will return to Him. We are created to be one. Yes, we can still be individual little balls rolling around on this Earth, but we are being drawn back to oneness. One day we will be one with God and each other. It is called unity.

Unity – complete oneness – will happen at the End of Time when we become one with God and each other, the Body of Christ, the Bride of Christ. But God wants us to express that one-ness now. In fact, the Bible says the world will know we are Christians by our love, by our unity. Our faith melds us together. In oneness, we prefer each other over ourselves. We give ourselves to the other. We help each other. We serve each other. We hurt with each other. We rejoice with each other. We are One.

Day 82: Why Love?

John 17:22-26

The Goal Is Unity

I am selfish. It is so easy to be selfish. We come by it so naturally. I have no problem thinking about me, about what I want, about what I think I need. Have you found it is so much easier to be self-centered than to be other-centered? To make decisions based on what benefits only you? To live Life without much thought of how your actions impact another? The problem is: this does not bring God glory.

In His prayer for us, Jesus expressed His concern about this:

> "I have given the the glory You gave Me so they may be one as We are One. I am in them and You are in Me. May they experience such perfect unity that the world will know that You sent Me and that You love them as much as You love Me. Father, I want these whom You have given Me to be with Me where I am. Then they can see all the gloryYou gave Me because You loved Me even before the world began!
>
> "O righteous Father, the world doesn't know You, but I do; and these disciples know You sent Me. I have revealed You to them and I will continue to do so.

Then Your love for Me will be in them, and I will be in them."

John 17:22-26

Glory is about perfection. God is perfect in love, in justice, truth, grace, compassion, mercy, and power. He is glorious. As we give room to His Spirit to work in us, He comes through us in how we love and live. The by-product of every believer letting God have His way in our life is unity.

Unity comes when everyone works to let God's glory come out of us. Unity is most readily recognized as love. Believers loving each other most accurately brings glory to God because God is love.

Warren Wiersbe says:

There is every reason why believers should love one another and live in unity. We trust the same Savior and share the same glory. We will one day enjoy the same Heaven! We belong to the same Father, and seek to do the same work, witnessing to a lost world that Jesus Christ alone saves from sin.

We believe the same truth, even though we may have different views of minor doctrinal matters, and we follow the same example that Jesus set for His people, to live a holy life. Yes, believers do have their

> *differences, but we have much more in common, and this should encourage us to love one another and promote true spiritual unity.*

It goes against every fiber of our human nature to love. Good thing God gave us a new nature!

Day 83: Garden Time

John 18:1-11

Where the Battle Is Won

I remember a painful time when I did not want to be married any more to my wife. I had been hurt in our relationship, and she had been hurt as well. We damaged and failed each other. There had been lies and unfaithfulness. It seemed like our love was dead and over.

In the middle of this, God said to me, *"Kurt, if you say you love Me, then you must choose to love your wife."* That was my "Garden moment." The Garden was where the decision was made to love ... and the battle was won in my mind. What followed was three years of intense counseling, where I learned to die to myself and to love like Jesus.

> After saying these things, Jesus crossed the Kidron Valley with His disciples and entered a grove of olive trees. Judas, the betrayer, knew this place because Jesus had often gone there with His disciples. The leading priests and Pharisees had given Judas a contingent of Roman soldiers and Temple guards to accompany him. Now, with blazing torches, lanterns and weapons, they arrived at the olive grove.
>
> Jesus fully realized all that was going to happen to Him, so He stepped forward to

meet them. "Who are you looking for?" He asked.

"Jesus the Nazarene," they replied.

"I AM He," Jesus said. (Judas, who betrayed Him, was standing with them.) As Jesus said, "I Am He," they all drew back and fell to the ground. Once more He asked them, "Who are you looking for?"

And again they replied, "Jesus the Nazarene."

"I told you that I AM He," Jesus said. "And since I am the One you want, let these others go." He did this to fulfill His own statement: "I did not lose a single one of those You have given Me."

Then Simon Peter drew a sword and slashed off the right ear of Malchus, the High Priest's slave. But Jesus said to Peter, "Put your sword back into its sheath. Shall I not drink from the cup of suffering the Father has given Me?"

John 18:1-11

Jesus fully realized all that was going to happen to Him, so He stepped forward to meet the soldiers. Picture this scene: dozens, perhaps hundreds of soldiers there to take Him. He does not run, He does not hide. He steps forward. And they shrink back and fall to the ground!

Could it be that when Jesus said, *"I AM He,"* that a wave of majestic power went out of Him and overwhelmed His enemies? I think for a moment, God was revealed to the soldiers. The point is, He did not have to go to His death. Like He said, *"No one takes My life from Me. I give it willingly."*

"I give it willingly." Those are words I would like to live better. There are two basic ways to approach relationships:

- ❖ The attitude that people are taking my life from me, so I resist giving it. This attitude causes me to live in the bondage of resentment and bitterness, always feeling like people are taking advantage of me.

OR

- ❖ I can embrace the truth that my life is mine to give, so I give it. No strings attached. It is my life to lay down, no one takes it from me, I choose to give it. This perspective brings freedom because – if it is mine to give – I need nothing in return. I choose to give. I give love freely.

The key to giving life willingly is the time we spend in the Garden with God. John does not tell us of Jesus' time of struggle in the Garden with His Father, but Matthew, Mark and Luke do. When

Jesus was wrestling with the knowledge of what He was facing, He asked His Father if possible to *"take this cup of suffering from Me"* (see Matthew 26:39, Mark 14:36, Luke 22:42). To release Him from the situation. Then, in the Garden, He settled the issue that He would indeed give His life willingly for the sake of love and relationship. He made the decision in the Garden to give His life away for those God had given Him. So when the time came to face the soldiers, He had **already** given Himself through love.

We win the struggle for relationships in the Garden with the Father. That is where we decide to give our life away to those God has given to us. It is in the Garden, time talking it over with God, where we settle the matter, make the decision to love and gain strength from the Father to lay down our life, our needs, our expectations. We decide ahead of time so when the time comes, we can give it willingly.

Oh, I wish it was easy! Sometimes it does feel like dying, does it not? When you love and do not feel loved? That is when it is so freeing, if you can, like Jesus, live from the truth: *"No one takes my life from me. I give it willing."*

Day 84: *"That One Man ..."*

John 18:12-14

One Choice

Finally, Jesus is alone, facing His enemies, His captors. The disciples have scattered and left Him, except for Peter who follows at a distance. The soldiers and Jewish leaders take Jesus to the house of the former High Priest, who had once prophesied unintentionally about Jesus:

> So the soldiers, their commanding officer and the Temple guards arrested Jesus and tied Him up. First they took Him to Annas, the father-in-law of Caiaphas, the High Priest at that time. Caiaphas was the one who had told the other Jewish leaders,"It's better that one Man should die for the people."
>
> **John 18:12-14**

It is all a matter of perspective: which side of Jesus are you for? Is Jesus a Friend ... or do you resist Him? Caiaphas was a resistor of Christ; he did not want to give in to God and change his ways. Caiaphas said these words, *"It is better that one Man should die"* because he wanted to protect his way of life.

Caiaphas knew he was breaking the Law by questioning Jesus without witnesses. He knew they were going to break the Law by putting an innocent man to death. But he had heard the crowds just a few days before, cheering for Jesus, and Caiaphas felt his own power slipping away. He had seen Jesus clear the Temple from the money-changers. So he put the plan in motion that *"one Man should die,"* but it really was not for the people – it was for power, it was for pride. Jesus would die, and they would be rid of a problem, a threat to their way of life.

God also said these words, *"That one Man should die"* through prophets of the Old Testament, and also through Paul:

> For the sin of this one man, Adam, caused death to rule over many. But even greater is God's wonderful grace and His gift of righteousness, for all who receive it will triumph over sin and death through this One Man, Jesus Christ. Yes, Adam's sin brings condemnation for everyone; but Christ's one act of righteousness brings a right relationship with God and new life for everyone.
>
> **Romans 5:17-18**

That One Man should die. Good news to those who accept – judgment for those who refuse.

Day 85: What the Rooster Said

John 18:15-27

A Study In Contrasts

I grew up on a small hobby-farm with all kinds of animals. We had goats, cats, dogs, chickens, cows, a horse, rabbits. We had a rooster for a little while. He was a small rooster, but he made a lot of noise. I can remember being awoken by him many times while it was still dark out, maybe 3 or 4 o'clock in the morning. I guess he did not know how to adjust to Daylight Savings Time. As far as I know, his crowing meant only one thing: *"I am ALIVE!!"*

One morning. the crowing abruptly stopped at about 4:00am. The bird had been crowing on and on – then I heard the back door slam. Then I heard ... nothing. My dad finally had enough of being awoken in the middle of the night and had whacked the bird. We had chicken for dinner.

Unlike our rooster, the rooster that crowed in the early morning of Jesus' arrest and Peter's denial of his Savior and Friend apparently had a lot to say.

> Simon Peter followed Jesus, as did another of the disciples. That other disciple was acquainted with the High Priest, so he was allowed to enter the High Priest's courtyard with Jesus.

Peter had to stay outside the gate. Then the disciple who knew the High Priest spoke to the woman watching at the gate, and she let Peter in. The woman asked Peter, "You're not one of that Man's disciples, are you?"

"No," he said, "I am not." Because it was cold, the household servants and the guards had made a charcoal fire. They stood around it, warming themselves, and Peter stood with them, warming himself.

Inside, the High Priest began asking Jesus about His followers and what He had been teaching them. Jesus replied, "Everyone knows what I teach. I have preached regularly in the synagogues and the Temple, where the people gather. I have not spoken in secret. Why are you asking Me this question? Ask those who heard Me. They know what I said."

Then one of the Temple guards standing nearby slapped Jesus across the face. "Is that the way to answer the High Priest?" he demanded.

Jesus replied, "If I said anything wrong, you must prove it. But if I'm speaking the truth, why are you beating Me?"

Then Annas bound Jesus and sent Him to Caiaphas, the High Priest. Meanwhile, as Simon Peter was standing by the fire warming himself, they asked him again, "You're not one of His disciples, are you?"

He denied it, saying, "No, I am not."

But one of the household slaves of the High Priest, a relative of the man whose ear Peter had cut off, asked, "Didn't I see you out there in the olive grove with Jesus?" Again Peter denied it. And immediately a rooster crowed.

John 18:15-27

The first thing to notice is that while Peter was outside denying his Savior, Jesus was inside taking a beating to protect His followers. The leaders wanted names and confessions so that they could also arrest his whole group of followers, but Jesus would not give them up. He took the punishment and took full responsibility for being God, and protected his own. That is the difference between God and Man. God remains true to us even while we are denying Him by the way we live.

"And the cock crowed." Think of all that was happening as even the rooster did his part like Jesus had predicted:

* The rooster crowed **assurance.** Assurance to Peter that Jesus was totally in control of the situation, even though He was bound and being harassed by the authorities. It was as if Jesus was saying, *"Remember, Peter, even this is part of the plan. I told you this would happen. I am in control."* By using one bird, Jesus affirmed His sovereignty and encouraged Peter, His follower.

* The rooster crowed **repentance.** It reminded Peter what Jesus had said, *"When you have come through the time of testing, turn to your companions and give them a fresh start"* (Luke 22:32). Luke tells us that Jesus turned and looked at Peter (see Luke 22:61), and this look of love broke Peter's heart. Peter had been a witness of Christ's sufferings (see 1 Peter 5:1); and by his own denials, he added to those sufferings.

* The rooster crowed of **new beginnings,** the announcement of the dawning of a new day! *"Weeping may last through the night, but joy comes with the morning"* (Psalm 30:5).

It is worthwhile to contrast Peter and Judas. Peter wept over his sins and repented – while Judas admitted his sins but never really repented. Judas experienced remorse, not repentance. When Judas went out from the Upper Room, *"it was night"* (John 13:30) – but when Peter went out to weep bitterly, there was the dawning of a new day. It is the contrast between godly sorrow that leads to true repentance, and the sorrow of the world (regret and remorse) that leads to death (see 2 Corinthians 7:9-10). We will discover that Jesus restored Peter (see John 21) and enabled him to serve with great power and blessing.

The night the rooster crowed, he announced both guilt and grace. Peter was guilty of resisting God's will – Judas was guilty of the worst kind of treachery. The mob was guilty of rejecting the Son of God and treating Him as though He were the lowest kind of criminal.

Jesus was full of grace, and the rooster had to crow!

(Thanks to Warren Wiersbe for his insight.)

Day 86: How God Planned to Die

John 18:28-40

No Surprises

Don't you love it when you plan something ... and it actually goes the way you planned? I planned a special birthday surprise for my wife's 40th birthday: I flew in her best friend Fiona from Taiwan.

The plan was to have another friend pick up Fiona at the Seattle airport and then wait with her at her Bothell home. I took Gwen out on "a date" to Seattle, with a stop by our friend's house. Gwen walked in to the surprise of her life: her good friend Fiona was there to hug her!

Everything went perfectly to the plan, and Gwen could not have been more happy or surprised. Sometimes we forget that God perfectly planned Jesus' life, His death and His resurrection to the perfect day, hour and even minute.

> Jesus' trial before Caiaphas ended in the early hours of the morning. Then He was taken to the headquarters of the Roman Governor. His accusers didn't go inside because it would defile them, and they wouldn't be allowed to celebrate the Passover. So Pilate, the Governor, went

out to them and asked, “What is your charge against this Man?”

“We wouldn’t have handed Him over to you if He weren’t a criminal!” they retorted.

“Then take Him away and judge Him by your own Law,” Pilate told them.

“Only the Romans are permitted to execute someone,” the Jewish leaders replied. (This fulfilled Jesus’ prediction about the way He would die.)

John 18:28-32

Why did the Jews not just have Jesus assassinated? They could have simply hired someone to make Him disappear. Because we must always remember: **it was in God’s plan for Jesus to die, and to die on a certain day and in a certain way.** God is sovereign, even in the worst of circumstances. If the Jews *alone* judged Jesus and found Him guilty, He would have been killed by stoning; and God had already determined that the Son would be crucified (see John 3:14, 8:28, 12:32-33).

Remember the rich imagery of the story of Moses lifting up a bronze serpent for the people to look at, to be saved from the snakebites they received in the wilderness (see Numbers 21:8). God’s plan was for Jesus to bear the curse of the Law and become a curse for us; and in order to do this, He had to hang on a tree (see Deuteronomy 21:22-23; Galatians 3:13). Only the Roman government could carry out a crucifixion, so God even used the Romans to fulfill His plan. Every step of God's plan was carried out in perfect detail.

It was not the Jews or the Romans who were in control of this situation; it was God calling the shots from Heaven.

> Then Pilate went back into his headquarters and called for Jesus to be brought to him. "Are You the King of the Jews?" he asked Him.
>
> Jesus replied, "Is this your own question, or do others tell you about Me?"
>
> "Am I a Jew?" Pilate retorted. "Your own people and their leading priests brought You to me for trial. Why? What have You done?"
>
> Jesus answered, "My Kingdom is not an earthly kingdom. If it were, My followers would fight to keep Me from being handed over to the Jewish leaders. But My Kingdom is not of this world."
>
> Pilate said, "So You are a king?"
>
> Jesus responded, "You say I am a King. Actually, I was born and came into the

> world to testify to the truth. All who love the truth recognize that what I say is true."
>
> "What is truth?" Pilate asked. Then he went out again to the people and told them, "He is not guilty of any crime. But you have a custom of asking me to release one prisoner each year at Passover. Would you like me to release this 'King of the Jews'?"
>
> But they shouted back, "No! Not this Man, we want Barabbas!" (Barabbas was a revolutionary.)
>
> **John 18:33-40**

God's choice to have the Romans involved was planned so that Jesus was declared innocent. Think of it: the ruling Roman government declared Jesus l**egally innocent**, and still allowed Jesus to be executed. So even by the ruling world government, Jesus, the Ultimate Sacrificial Lamb, was declared free from defect. When this was over, people would know and remember that an innocent Man had died for their sins.

And what of Barabbas? Here was a man who was guilty of crimes against the Roman government. He was guilty and should have died for his crimes, but it was his lucky day when Jesus was arrested. The innocent God-Man took his place, and Barabbas went free. What an amazing subplot in this story, a subplot which tells the

Gospel in just a few lines: Man sins ... is scheduled to die ... God arrives ... takes Man's place ... Man goes free. That is the Gospel, that is the Good News. Because we are Barabbas.

Day 87: When God Suffered

John 19:1-16

Obliterating Pain

What is the worst pain you have endured? Did you have a baby? Guys, I have been told that the pain from passing kidney stones is comparable to giving birth. I do not know – I have never done either. Perhaps you have had appendicitis, or maybe you have battled cancer. My dad's fight with cancer was terribly painful.

When I was 10, I was riding on the back of a flat-bed truck with a hay-rack over the cab. I had to duck under the eaves when my uncle Pete drove the truck into the machine shed. It was not straight, so he backed out. In the meantime, I had stood up again ... and was dragged through the four-inch space between the hay-rack and the low eaves.

My shoulder blade got stuck in the space and was torn and broken. Then it was time for my head: my head was forced side-ways, and the thing I remember most about this accident – which took about 10 seconds – was the sound of my teeth breaking and grinding as my head was forced through a space too small for it. My ear was torn and bleeding.

I guess that accident hurt pretty badly ... but was nothing compared to what our Jesus endured.

Then Pilate had Jesus flogged with a lead-tipped whip. The soldiers wove a crown of thorns and put it on His head, and they put a purple robe on Him. "Hail! King of the Jews!" they mocked, as they slapped Him across the face.

Pilate went outside again and said to the people, "I am going to bring Him out to you now, but understand clearly that I find Him not guilty." Then Jesus came out wearing the crown of thorns and the purple robe. And Pilate said, "Look, here is the Man!"

When they saw Him, the leading priests and Temple guards began shouting, "Crucify Him! Crucify Him!"

"Take Him yourselves and crucify Him," Pilate said. "I find Him not guilty."

The Jewish leaders replied, "By our Law, He ought to die because He called Himself the Son of God"

When Pilate heard this, he was more frightened than ever. He took Jesus back into the headquarters again and asked Him, "Where are You from?" But Jesus gave no answer. "Why don't You talk to me?" Pilate demanded. "Don't You realize that I have the power to release You or crucify You?"

Then Jesus said, "You would have no power over Me at all unless it were given to you from above. So the one who handed Me over to you has the greater sin."

Then Pilate tried to release Him, but the Jewish leaders shouted, "If you release this Man, you are no 'friend of Caesar.' Anyone who declares Himself a King is a rebel against Caesar."

When they said this, Pilate brought Jesus out to them again. Then Pilate sat down on the Stone Pavement (in Hebrew, "Gabbatha"). It was about noon on the day of preparation for the Passover. And Pilate said to the people, "Look, here is your King!"

"Away with Him," they yelled. "Away with Him! Crucify Him!"

"What? Crucify your King?" Pilate asked.

"We have no king but Caesar," the leading priests shouted back. Then Pilate turned Jesus over to them to be crucified.

John 19:1-16

Hundreds of years before, Isaiah prophesied this would happen to Jesus, Messiah:

> He was despised and rejected - a Man of sorrows, acquainted with deepest grief. We turned our backs on Him and looked the other way. He was despised, and we did not care. Yet it was our weaknesses He carried; it was our sorrows that weighed Him down. And we thought His troubles were a punishment from God, a punishment for His own sins! But He was pierced for our rebellion, crushed for our sins. He was beaten so we could be whole. He was whipped so we could be healed. All of us, like sheep, have strayed away. We have left God's paths to follow our own. Yet the Lord laid on Him the sins of us all. He was oppressed and treated harshly, yet He never said a word. He was led like a lamb to the slaughter. And as a sheep is silent before the shearers, He did not open His mouth. Unjustly condemned, He was led away.
>
> **Isaiah 53:3-8**

Just let it sink in once more what Jesus went through for you and me.

Day 88: Crucifixion

John 19:17-27

When God Died

> So they took Jesus away. Carrying the cross by Himself, He went to the place called "Place of the Skull" (in Hebrew, "Golgotha"). They they nailed Him to the cross. Two others were crucified with Him, one on either side, with Jesus between them. And Pilate posted a sign over Him that read, "Jesus of Nazareth, the King of the Jews." The place where Jesus was crucified was near the city, and the sign was written in Hebrew, Latin and Greek, so that many people could read it.
>
> **John 19:17-20**

It was Passover, so thousands of pilgrims would pass by Golgotha and see Jesus hanging between two criminals, fulfilling Isaiah 53:12, *"He was numbered among transgressors."*

It is so impacting to remember and meditate what our Savior endured for us:

* He hung entirely naked in shame before men, women and children
* He hung in the company of common criminals, falsely accused and falsely condemned
* He hung wracked in the most intense pain imaginable, having already endured a night

and day of beating with instruments that were meant to leave him within a fraction of death.

He did this for you. He did this for me. It was the Plan.

> Then the leading priests objected and said to Pilate, "Change it from 'The King of the Jews' to 'He said, I am the King of the Jews.'"
>
> Pilate replied, "No, what I have written, I have written."
>
> When the soldiers had crucified Jesus, they divided His clothes among the four of them. They also took His robe, but it was seamless, woven in one piece from top to bottom. So they said, "Rather than tearing it apart, let's throw dice for it." This fulfilled the Scripture that says, "They divided My garments among themselves and threw dice for My clothing." So that is what they did.
>
> **John 19:21-24**

More prophecy fulfilled from Psalms 22:18, more confirmation that Jesus was God in the flesh. God had planned out this day; He knew exactly how it was going to happen. Even Pilate confirmed the truth by writing the legal description for Jesus' placard, for He really is the King of Kings and Lord of Lords.

Standing near the cross were Jesus' mother, His mother's sister, Mary (the wife of Clopas), and Mary Magdalene. When Jesus saw His mother standing there beside the disciple He loved, He said to her, "Dear woman, here is your son." And He said to this disciple, "Here is your mother." And from then on, this disciple took her into his home.

John 19:25-27

To the end, Jesus was taking care of the people He loved. His father Joseph had passed away, and so Jesus – being the oldest Son – was responsible for His mother. Amazing love, how can it be, that even in excruciating pain, Jesus would do the right thing and make arrangements for the care of His mother! Even in the midst of torturous death on the cross, He put the needs of others above His own.

This should encourage us. It is good to know that we can put our very hearts in the hands of Jesus, and He will take good care of us. He will make sure we, His children, receive all we need from Him.

Day 89: *"It Is Finished"*

John 19:28-30

The Mighty Warrior-God

> Jesus knew that His mission was now finished; and to fulfill Scripture, He said, "I am thirsty."
>
> **John 19:28**

By asking for a drink, Jesus was fulfilling the prophecy of Psalm 69:21, *"They offer Me sour wine for My thirst."* Other Gospel writers tell that Jesus had just emerged from three hours of darkness where He endured the wrath of God and experienced separation from His Father for the only time in eternity. If you think about it: God's wrath + isolation from God + never-ending thirst = Hell. Jesus was going through Hell so that we would not have to.

John goes on to tell us:

> A jar of sour wine was sitting there, so they soaked a sponge in it, put it on a hyssop branch, and held it up to His lips. When Jesus had tasted it, He said, "It is finished!" Then He bowed His head and released His Spirit.
>
> **John 19:29-30**

Other writers of the Gospels tell us that Jesus SHOUTED, *"It is finished!"* triumphantly. He was not going out as a defeated, defeated Man, but as a MIGHTY GOD-WARRIOR, doing warfare for the souls of His own beloved children.

Warren Wiersbe tells us:

This word telelestai *in Greek means,* "It is finished, it stands finished, and it always will be finished!" *While it is true that our Lord's sufferings were now finished, there is much more included in this dramatic word. Many of the Old Testament types and prophecies were now fulfilled, and the once-for-all sacrifice for sin had now been completed.*

The word telelestai *is unfamiliar to us, but it was used by various people in everyday life in those days. A servant would use it when reporting to his or her master,* "I have completed the work assigned to me" *(see John 17:4). When a priest examined an animal sacrifice and found it faultless, this word would apply. Jesus, of course, is the perfect Lamb of God, without spot or blemish. When an artist completed a picture, or a writer a manuscript, he or she might say, "It is finished!" The death of Jesus on the cross "completes the picture" that God had been painting, the story that He had been writing for centuries. Because of the cross, we understand the ceremonies and prophecies in the Old Testament.*

> *Perhaps the most meaningful meaning of* telelestai *was that used by the merchants:* "The debt is paid in full!" *When He gave Himself on the cross, Jesus fully met the righteous demands of a Holy Law; He paid our debt in full. None of the Old Testament sacrifices could take away sins; their blood only covered sin. But the Lamb of God shed His blood, and that blood can take away the sins of the world (see John 1:29; Hebrews 9:24-28).*

It is so impacting to remember God chose this weekend for Jesus to die. It was the Passover, the time when a perfect lamb, without blemish, was chosen to be offered for the sins of the people. Every Jew knew what this meant, and this day held tremendous significance for them. Remember the words of John the Baptist when he first identified Jesus as Savior, *"Behold the Lamb of God, Who takes away the sins of the world."* Jesus was that Lamb, the sacrifice for all sin, for all time.

For us, it meant that from this time forward we too, as Gentiles, would be given equal inheritance to the riches of forgiveness, cleansing, having our sins paid for, and being brought into relationship with our Creator. *"Jesus paid it all / All to Him we owe ...."*

Oh the wonderful cross, oh the wonderful cross
Bids me come and die, to find that I may truly live
Oh the wonderful cross, oh the wonderful cross

All who gather here by grace draw near and bless His name
Love so amazing, so divine
Demands my soul, my life, my all!

Day 90: Passover Lamb

John 19:31-37

Jesus On Task, On Time

Who was Jesus of Nazareth? He was God's own Passover Lamb, sacrificed for the sins of the world.

> It was the day of preparation, and the Jewish leaders didn't want the bodies hanging there the next day, which was the Sabbath (and a very special Sabbath because it was the Passover). So they asked Pilate to hasten their deaths by ordering that their legs be broken. Then their bodies could be taken down.
>
> **John 19:31**

The Jewish leaders were worried about Jesus lingering and hanging on to life until sundown, which would have been the beginning of the Sabbath. After sundown, of course, no work could be done by the Jews, and it would not be *kosher* (sorry for the pun) to have bodies hanging on a cross over Passover. The irony is amazing here; they would wrongly accuse and murder a Man, but could not have Him hanging around on the Sabbath. Incredible hypocrisy.

They did not have to worry about Jesus lingering: He was right on task, right on time. He gave up His Spirit, chose to breathe His last breath at precisely 3:00pm, just as the Father had planned.

The tradition of the Romans was to break the legs of any prisoner lingering, so that he could not brace himself and push up with his legs to breathe. He would then die almost immediately, unable to fill his lungs with air, suffocated by the weight of his body.

> So the soldiers came and broke the legs of the two men crucified with Jesus. But when they came to Jesus, they saw that He was already dead so they didn't break His legs. One of the soldiers, however, pierced His side with a spear, and immediately blood and water flowed out.
>
> **John 19:32-34**

Another amazing fulfillment of Scripture! The Roman soldiers actually broke protocol in two ways here so that Scripture could be fulfilled. They saw Jesus was dead, so they did not break His legs as they were ordered. This fulfilled prophecy in Psalm 34:20 that none of Jesus' bones would be broken – but also it fulfilled the commands God had given His people to never break the bones of the Passover lamb (see Exodus 12:46, Numbers 9:12).

You see, Jesus did not die to fulfill Passover – rather, **God designed Passover to celebrate what Jesus, the Passover Lamb, would fulfill.** He told the Jews never to break a bone in their sacrificial lambs because HE KNEW that Jesus' bones would not be broken. Amazing!

Protocol was broken the second time by the soldiers when they pierced Jesus' side. This was not the norm; soldiers knew better than this. They knew the force of the weight of the body would spray blood all over, and it would get on them. They were not commanded to pierce His side – but God had said that our Savior would be pierced (Zechariah 12:12), and so prophecy was once again fulfilled by an unlikely participant: a Roman soldier. God truly is sovereign. He is in control.

> (This report is from an eyewitness, giving an accurate account. He speaks the truth so that you also can believe.) These things happened in fulfillment of the Scriptures that say, "Not one of His bones will be broken," and "They will look on the One they pierced."
>
> **John 19:35-37**

Warren Wiersbe tells us:

John saw a special significance to the blood and water that came from the wound in the side. For one thing, it proved that Jesus had a real body (see 1 John 1:1-4) and experienced a real death. By the time John wrote this book, there were false teachers in the Church claiming that Jesus did not have a truly human body.

There may also be a symbolic meaning: the blood speaks of our justification, the water of our sanctification and cleansing.

> *The blood takes care of the guilt of sin ... the water deals with the stain of sin. Some students connect John 19:34 with 1 John 5:6, but perhaps the connection is weak. In 1 John 5, John deals with evidence that Jesus Christ is God come in the flesh; and He presents three witnesses: the Spirit, the water, and the blood (see 1 John 5:6, 8). The Spirit relates to Pentecost, the water to His baptism, and the blood to His crucifixion. In each of these events, God made it clear that Jesus Christ is what He claimed to be, God come in the flesh. In fact, in John 19:35, the apostle makes it clear that the water and blood should encourage his readers to believe that Jesus is the Christ (see John 20:31).*

Remember: whenever we are being pierced by any sword in this life, that our Father is with us. Even to the death. He is in control.

Day 91: Jesus' Friends

John 19:38-42

About Joe and Nick

Sometimes we get the idea that the only people who followed Jesus were the down-and-outers. That is just not true. Jesus influenced some pretty high-powered people in Jewish circles. He even had followers in the Sanhedrin and on the Jewish High Council. Check it out:

> Afterward, Joseph of Arimathea, who had been a secret disciple of Jesus (because he feared the Jewish leaders), asked Pilate for permission to take down Jesus' body. When Pilate gave permission, Joseph came and took the body away.
>
> **John 19:38**

What do we know about Joseph of Arimathea? John informs us that Joseph was a *"secret disciple for fear of the Jews."* The Greek word translated *"secretly"* is a perfect passive participle and could be translated *"having been secreted."* In Matthew 13:35, this same verb form is translated *"have been kept secret."* In other words, Joseph was God's "secret agent" in the Sanhedrin! From the human standpoint, Joseph kept "under cover" because he feared the Jews (John 7:13, 9:22, 12:42) – but from the divine standpoint, he was being protected so he could be available to bury the body of Jesus.

We also know that Joseph was rich (see Matthew 27:57), a prominent member of the Jewish council (see Mark 15:43) ... a good and righteous man who had not consented to what the Council did (see Luke 23:50-51) ... a member of that "believing minority" of Jews who were praying for Messiah to come (see Mark 15:43; and note Luke 2:25-38) ... and a disciple of Jesus Christ (John 19:38).

> With him came Nicodemus, the man who had come to Jesus at night. He brought 75 pounds of perfumed ointment made from myrrh and aloes.
>
> **John 19:39**

We have already met Nicodemus in our study of John. Note that each time he is named, he is identified as the man who came to Jesus by night (Nick at Night; see John 3:1-20; 7:50-53). But the man who started off with confusion at night (John 3) ended up with open confession in the daylight!

Nicodemus came out of the dark and into the light and – with Joseph of Arimathea – was not ashamed to publicly identify with Jesus Christ. Of course, when the two men touched His dead body, they defiled themselves and could not participate in Passover. But what difference did it make? They had found the Lamb of God!

> Following Jewish burial custom, they wrapped Jesus' body with the spices, in long sheets of linen cloth. The place of

> crucifixion was near a garden where there was a new tomb, never used before. And so, because it was the day of preparation for the Jewish Passover and since the tomb was close at hand, they laid Jesus there.
>
> **John 19:40-42**

All of this raises the question, *"How did Joseph and Nicodemus know to prepare for His burial?"* Warren Wiersbe says:

> *What follows is only conjecture on my part but, to me, it seems reasonable. When Nicodemus first visited Jesus, he was impressed with His miracles and His teachings; but he could not understand what it meant to be born again. Certainly after that interview, Nicodemus searched the Scriptures and asked God for guidance concerning these important spiritual matters.*
>
> *At the critical Council meeting recorded in John 7:45-53, Nicodemus boldly stood up and defended the Savior! His associates ridiculed him for thinking that a prophet could come out of Galilee!* "Search, and look!" *they said – and that is exactly what Nicodemus did.*
>
> *It is likely that Joseph of Arimathea quietly joined him, and revealed the fact that he too was more and more convinced that Jesus*

of Nazareth was indeed Israel's Messiah, the Son of God. As Nicodemus and Joseph searched the Old Testament, they would find the messianic prophecies and discover that many of them had been fulfilled in Jesus Christ. Certainly they would see Him as the "Lamb of God" and conclude that He would be sacrificed at Passover.

Jesus had already told Nicodemus that He would be "lifted up" *(John 3:14), and this meant crucifixion. Since the Passover lambs were slain about 3:00pm, the two men could know almost the exact time when God's Lamb would die on the cross!*

Surely they would read Isaiah 53 and notice verse 9: "And He made His grave with the wicked, and with the rich in His death." *Jesus would be buried in a rich man's tomb! Joseph arranged to have the tomb hewn out, and the men assembled the cloths and spices needed for the burial. They may have been hiding in the tomb all during the six hours of our Lord's agony on the cross.*

When they heard, "It is finished! Father, into Thy hands I commend My spirit!" – *they knew that He was dead, and they went to work. They boldly identified with Jesus Christ at a time when He seemed like a failure and His cause hopelessly defeated. As far as we know, of all the disciples, only John was with them at the cross.*

> *The Sabbath was about to dawn. Jesus had finished the work of the* “new creation” *(2 Corinthians 5:17), and now He would rest.*

It is so awesome to see all the people God used: from simple soldiers ... to the Roman governor ... to members of the high Jewish Council – all to accomplish His plan. We serve a truly sovereign God!

Day 92: Faith Sees

John 20:1-10

The Bridge of Faith

Have you ever lost someone you really loved? Someone who believed in you and cheered you on to greatness? When we have been loved deeply and unconditionally by someone, we want to be near them. It is hard to let them go because we have been so deeply impacted by their influence and presence. Life feels empty and we feel alone, and it is hard to believe they could really be gone.

I am fairly sure Mary just could not bear to be away from her Savior – she just wanted to be near Him.

> Early on Sunday morning while it was still dark, Mary Magdalene came to the tomb and found that the stone had been rolled away from the entrance. She ran and found Simon Peter and the other disciple, the one whom Jesus loved. She said, "They have taken the Lord's body out of the tomb, and we don't know where they have put Him!"
>
> **John 20:1**

Imagine her shock and confusion when she goes, expecting to find the One she loved Who is now dead, then she is all set to prepare His body for burial ... and He is not there! You see, Jesus' followers still did not understand He was going to rise again. They were still engulfed in the grief and shock of seeing their Friend die an excruciating death on the cross.

Jesus had told His followers many times that He would rise from the dead. This idea was not new to them; they had actually seen it occur when Lazarus came forth from the tomb after being dead for several days. It was not out of the realm of possibility for them. But their eyes of faith were blinded by fear and grief.

Fear and grief are grave robbers, faith robbers, robbers of possibility, robbers of potential, robbers of truth. Fear is the emotion we give way to when we think we may lose something very important to us ... and grief is the emotion we experience when we perceive we have lost what was important already. Both fear and grief blind us from seeing what God wants us to see; both block faith.

> Peter and the other disciple started out for the tomb. They were both running, but the other disciple outran Peter and reached the tomb first. He stooped and looked in, and saw the linen wrappings lying there, but he didn't go in. Then Simon peter arrived and went inside. He also noticed the linen wrappings lying there, while the cloth that had covered Jesus' head was folded up and lying apart from the other wrappings.
>
> Then the disciple who had reached the tomb first also went in, and he saw and

> believed – for until then, they still hadn't understood the Scriptures that said Jesus must rise from the dead. Then they went home.
>
> **John 20:3-10**

Faith is a progression of God's faithfulness; faith is built. Sometimes we do not see the big picture all at once – but as we keep seeking God, drawing close to Him, searching for His big picture, we see. Our seeing increases by seeking – and we see when we seek.

In verse 5, John says he looked from a distance, from outside the door, and *"saw the linen wrappings lying there."* The Greek word he used for *"saw"* is *"to glance or look in."* In verse 6, when Peter went inside or got closer, the word John used for *"saw"* is *"to look carefully, to observe."* When we draw close and pay attention to what God is doing, we begin to see His hand at work, and faith is built. In verse 8, when John decides to get as close as he can to what God is doing and draws near to where Jesus was, he says he *"saw and believed."* The word he uses for *"saw"* is *"to perceive with intelligent comprehension."* What God had accomplished was beginning to *"dawn on him."*

God's purpose for Jesus' death was beginning to be seen and understood. The lights were coming on. Remember, these friends of Jesus had just finished celebrating the Passover; it was fresh in their minds. Do you suppose finding the grave-clothes empty would have reminded them of the Passover tradition where the parents hide the *afikomen* (dessert *matzo*), and the children search for it until they find it? The simple truth is that God's ways are not Man's ways.

What Man sees as fearful and grief-filled, God is already working in for His purposes and His glory. The bridge between Man's perspective and God's perspective is faith. Faith is believing that no matter how dark the circumstances, God is good and is working out His good will in us. The more we seek to see, the more we will believe in His goodness.

Day 93: Knowing God

John 20:11-18

When God Speaks My Name

I was in Haiti visiting the orphans supported by our church family. As usual in the morning, we were hanging out, talking and playing on the porch of the clinic. I had been reading my Bible and writing in my journal. Emanuel – the boy our *Kids Place* supports – motioned that he wanted to use my pen.

Taking my big white hand in his small brown hand, he painstakingly wrote his name – EMANUEL – on the palm of my hand. I asked Herby, our interpreter, to ask Emanuel why had had written his name on my hand. The answer came quickly: *"When you go back home, I do not want you to forget about me. I want you to remember my name."*

> Mary was standing outside the tomb crying, and as she wept, she stooped and looked inside. She saw two white-robed angels, one sitting at the head and the other at the foot of the place where the body of Jesus had been lying, "Dear woman, why are you crying?" the angels asked her.
>
> "Because they have taken away my Lord," she replied, "and I don't know where they have put Him."
>
> **John 20:11-13**

Still Mary was seeking, looking, grieving the loss of her Friend and Lord, the One Who had accepted her unconditionally and treated her, a woman, with respect. In the Jewish culture, women were little more than slaves, and were not given much social status whatsoever. But Jesus did not pay attention to social morés: He valued and treated each person as He knew them to be – as a precious child of God.

When Mary looked into the tomb, she saw the angels through her tears, and must have thought they were men. In any case, they were not who she was looking for, so she turned away from them. She was not seeking angels – she was seeking Jesus.

> She turned to leave and saw someone standing there. It was Jesus, but she didn't recognize Him. "Dear woman, why are you crying?" Jesus asked her. "Who are you looking for?"
>
> She thought He was the gardener. "Sir," she said, "if you have taken Him away, tell me where you have put Him, and I will go and get Him."
>
> **John 20:14-15**

Mary was committed to find Jesus and give Him a proper burial. She knew that a couple of men had prepared His body, and probably figured they had not done a good job. She wanted to take proper time and care, and make sure that Jesus' body was prepared perfectly for burial. She wanted to see Him one last time, to minister to Him one last time. She deeply loved her Savior.

Again, through her tears and in the darkness of the early morning, she failed to recognize it was Jesus to Whom she was speaking. She was beside herself with grief ... and in the Middle East when someone cried, they wailed loudly and passionately. She had seen Jesus die on the cross; she was not expecting to see Him alive, but laying on the bench, lifeless.

Perhaps Jesus veiled His appearance so that she wouldn't recognize Him immediately, or perhaps in His risen state, He looked different enough that she just did not know Him. However, when He spoke her name ....

> "Mary!" Jesus said.
>
> She turned to Him and cried out, "Rabboni!" (which is Hebrew for "Teacher").
>
> "Don't cling to Me," Jesus said, "for I haven't yet ascended to the Father. But go find My brothers and tell them, 'I am ascending to My Father and your Father, to My God and your God.'"
>
> Mary Magdalene found the disciples and told them, "I have seen the Lord!" Then

she gave them His message.

John 20:16-18

All Jesus had to do was speak her name, and Mary knew Him. Remember, Jesus had told His friends in John 10:3, *"His sheep would recognize His voice and come to Him. He calls His own sheep by name, and leads them out."* She heard her Master speak her name, and she recognized it was Jesus. No one knows us like Jesus.

God knows your name. In knowing your name, He knows every detail about you. You are His own child, and He definitely has your best interests in mind. Do you believe that? If you believe, then more and more you want to know Him, to be with Him, to understand His heart and will.

Knowing God gives way to obedience in your heart. Mary wanted to do nothing else at that moment than to cling to Jesus; she did not ever want to lose Him again. She just wanted to stay with Him, enjoy the security of being in the presence of the One Who loved her like no other.

Makes sense, right? But Jesus said to her, *"Go find My brothers and tell them."* So she did. Obedience was Mary's expression of love to Jesus. It is how she said back to Him, *"I love You."*

Obedience is still our way of telling Jesus we love Him. If we ever wonder whether we really love God, just practice obedience to His Word. His Word says in 1 John 5:3, *"This is love for God: to obey His commands."* What is His most basic command? Love others enough to go tell them, "I have seen the Lord."

God is speaking your name. Do you recognize His voice?

Day 94: When I Am Afraid

John 20:19-23

Peace Overcomes Fear

Do you ever feel afraid? Anxious? Perhaps even depressed because of the stress this world puts upon you? Everyone struggles with fear at some point, and the disciples were no different. Passover was over – and here they were, on Sunday, once more fearing for their lives. They were afraid of what men might do to them.

> That Sunday evening, the disciples were meeting behind locked doors because they were afraid of the Jewish leaders. Suddenly, Jesus was standing them among them! "Peace be with you," He said.
>
> **John 20:19**

When I am afraid, Jesus comes to me. He brings peace into my circumstances. He brings my focus back to him. Peace is to know God is in control, He is sovereign in my life. Peace is to know that – like the cross – this too will pass. Jesus is with me through any difficulty that comes my way. So I do not have to give in to fear. I can have peace. The Prince of Peace is with me so, "Peace, be with me."

> As He spoke, He showed them the wounds in His hands and His side. They

were filled with joy when they saw the Lord!"

John 20:20

When I am afraid, Jesus reassures me. His wounds remind me that the worst thing men can do to me is kill my body, but can never touch my soul, the Eternal part of me. He reminds me that what I fear will not even exist when this life is over. This life is but a speck on the timeline of Eternity, because Eternity is timeless. He helps me live in the bigger picture: His will, His plans. His reassurance is that – no matter what happens in my life – He is with me and will get me through it. At the end of the day, it is me and Jesus.

Again He said, "Peace be with you. As the Father has sent Me, so I am sending you." Then He breathed on them and said, "Receive the Holy Spirit."

John 20:21-22

When I am afraid, Jesus reassures me. He gives me the Holy Spirit, Who gives me courage and authority to make great decisions when fear strikes. He enables me to do the right thing and to hold to the convictions He has given. Even though I may be tempted to take the easy way out of fear, He enables me to take the right way out of fear. *"Like a roadway in the wilderness, He leads us."*

"If you forgive anyone's sins, they are forgiven. If you do not forgive them, they are not forgiven."

John 20:23

When I am afraid, Jesus commissions me. It is important to understand the way this verse works in the Greek. The late Greek scholar Dr. Julius R. Mantey says that the correct translation both here and in Matthew 16:19 should be:

> *"Whosoever sins you remit (forgive) shall have already been forgiven them, and whosoever sins you retain (do not forgive) shall have already not been forgiven them."*

In other words, the disciples did not provide forgiveness; they **proclaimed** forgiveness on the basis of the message of the Gospel. Another Greek scholar, Dr. Kenneth Wuest, translates it: *"They have been previously forgiven them."*

As the early believers went forth into the world, they announced the good news of salvation. If sinners would repent and believe on Jesus Christ, their sins would be forgiven them! *"Who can forgive sins but God only?"* (Mark 2:7). All that the Christian can do is announce the message of forgiveness; God performs the miracle of forgiveness. If sinners will believe on Jesus Christ, we can authoritatively declare to them that their sins have been forgiven; but we are not the ones who provide the forgiveness.

We battle fear by proclaiming forgiveness. We have a higher calling than to live in fear. Our calling is to proclaim freedom through forgiveness.

God speaks our names – do we recognize His voice?

Day 95: Blind Faith

John 20:24-29

God Is Always Good

While we were living in Taiwan, my wife had laser surgery on her eyes. She rode with some friends to the clinic because they had made a deal: to buy ten procedures and get one procedure for free (only in Taiwan!). I agreed to pick her up when she was ready.

Without thinking, I hopped on our scooter and rode across Taichung to get her. I never considered what it would be like for her to endure the 25-minute ride home in Taichung's rush-hour traffic, on the back of a scooter, her eyes bandaged closed and entirely blind. I am not known as the best driver in the world, and in Taiwan, you have to be very aggressive to stay alive in the sea of scooters and crazy drivers.

She told me later she was terrified as she hung on for dear life – the horns, the smells, the exhaust, the brush-ups pressing in on her from every direction. She really had to trust me.

It all comes down to faith, does it not? Believing Jesus is God, I mean. Putting our hope in Him. Sometimes it can be hard to believe. We see this world around us, and may wonder, *"Where is God?"* Or tragedy strikes in our lives or the life of someone we love, and we ask that ancient question, *"Why?"* Or we face a hard time for a long time, and we cannot see **how** God is ever going to help us. Faith means believing Jesus Christ is God, and that God is good and at work, even when we cannot see the outcome. Even people who lived and walked with Jesus struggled in their faith.

> One of the twelve disciples, Thomas (nicknamed the Twin), was not with the others when Jesus came. They told him, "We have seen the Lord!"
>
> But he replied, "I won't believe it unless I see the nail wounds in His hands, put my fingers into them, and place my hand into the wound in His side."
>
> **John 20:24-25**

Would it not be great to have all our questions answered? Then we could say without the shadow of a doubt, *"Okay, now I see!"* If we could see and touch Jesus, bring Him around to meet our friends, take Him to small group and have Him do a miracle or two, would not that be great? Well, that would also not be faith. And God's whole plan for us coming to Him revolves around faith. Why? Because faith levels the playing field of life. Anyone and everyone can choose to believe. God loves faith, and He loves people who choose to live in simple, trusting faith.

> Eight days later, the disciples were together again and this time Thomas was with them. The doors were locked; but suddenly, as before, Jesus was

standing among them. "Peace be with you," He said.

Then He said to Thomas, "Put your finger here and look at My hands. Put your hand into the wound in My side. Don't be faithless any longer. Believe!"

"My Lord and my God!" Thomas exclaimed.

John 20:26-28

For some reason Jesus chose to help Thomas one more time in his faith. He gave Thomas what he asked for: a physical touch. Then Jesus told him to believe. The literal translation of Jesus' words are: *"Stop becoming faithless but become a believer."*

Faith is built by choosing, time after time, to believe. It is built primarily by letting the Holy Spirit sear the Truth of His Word into our beliefs and our thoughts. Our belief is proven by the action we take because of our faith. Sometimes God chooses to help us build our faith -- He gives us a touch or a moment of revelation. I have had times when God has shown Himself to me through an undeniable healing, or a powerful physical feeling from Him. I have heard His reassuring voice come into my thoughts, and have lived out prophetic words spoken over my life. These are all faith-builders, but for the most part I live out long stretches of time by faith, simply believing. I cannot see Him, but I simply choose to believe in

Him. Jesus loves and blesses people who believe without seeing Him, believing blindly, you might say.

> Then Jesus told him, "You believe because you have seen Me. Blessed are those who believe without seeing Me."
>
> **John 20:29**

Day 96: *"You Just Had to Be There"*

John 20:30-31

The Untold Stories

"You just had to be there." How many times have we heard those words? We can tell the story the best way possible, we can fill in every detail, but to really catch the richness and fullness of the story we tell our listeners, *"You just had to be there."*

Imagine the stories that have not been told about Jesus – the things He said and did that did not make it into the Gospels! Volumes could have been written about the hours of every day of the three years the disciples walked with Jesus. Imagine all the "smaller but still significant" stories that happened along the way. Would not you love to sit around a campfire with the disciples and hear all the stuff that did not get into the Gospels?

> The disciples saw Jesus do many other miraculous signs in addition to the ones recorded in this book. But these are written so that you may continue to believe that Jesus is the Messiah, the Son of God; and that by believing in Him, you will have life by the power of His Name.
>
> **John 20:30-31**

It is not the miracles that make us believe. Lots of people saw Jesus do miracles ... and lots of people still did not believe. The miracles only draw our attention, but then it is the Spirit of God that captures our heart and convinces us to believe that Jesus is God. Miracles simply lead us to His Word, where we are filled with Truth which leads to Life. Miracles are just the first step toward faith in Jesus.

You see, its not about the miracles – it is about the God-Man, Jesus the Christ. The truly significant miracle is when, by believing in the Son of God, our lives are transformed. We believe and become eternal children of God. A miracle takes place which changes Eternity – because when we believe, we become eternal. For each of us who believe, another vibrant color of thread is woven into the tapestry of Heaven. We have Life by the power of His Name.

Day 97: Waiting For God

John 21:1-7

Ask Jesus

I hate waiting. Sometimes my lovely wife tells me she will be ready in 5 minutes, but guess what? Her "5 minutes" is different than my "5 minutes." So what do I do? I sit at the piano and play, or I play Apps on my iPhone, or I read.

What do you do while you are waiting? We tend to go back to what we are most comfortable doing. We tend to go back to what we know best. After Jesus rose from the dead, He told His disciples to meet Him at Galilee, so they were waiting for Jesus.

Presumably, Peter got tired of waiting ....

> Later, Jesus appeared again to the disciples beside the Sea of Galilee. This is how it happened.
>
> Several of the disciples were there - Simon Peter, Thomas (nicknamed the Twin), Nathanael from Cana in Galilee, the sons of Zebedee, and two other disciples. Simon Peter said, "I'm going fishing."
>
> "We'll come too," they all said. So they went out in the boat, but they caught nothing all night.

At dawn, Jesus was standing on the beach, but the disciples couldn't see Who He was. He called out, "Fellows, have you caught any fish?"

"No," they replied.

Then He said, "Throw out your net on the right-hand side of the boat, and you'll get some!" So they did ... and they couldn't haul in the net because there were so many fish in it.

Then the disciple Jesus loved said to Peter, "It's the Lord!"

John 21:1-7

Jesus was about to remind His disciples of a few main truths before He left them to go back to Heaven:

Truth #1: Life does not work without Jesus. Was Peter discouraged again, quickly frustrated by the fact Jesus was not showing up? Was there a sense of *"Forget this!"* in his statement, as in: *"Forget this waiting stuff. I am going fishing!"* Was there a tone in his voice like: *"I can take care of myself. I am going to do what I am good at, what I know I can do!"*?

When we wait for God, we can be tempted to do things our own way, to make things happen, to "take care of business." Sometimes we make decisions while we wait that are fruitless, and get us into even more trouble. Our self-centered decisions can pile yet another layer of complication upon our already complicated circumstances. Sometimes God just wants us to wait and trust.

It is worth noting that Jesus lets His disciples make this decision. Then Jesus makes a point of letting His disciples know that **He knows** they have not caught anything. He makes them admit they were unsuccessful without Him. When He knows they have acknowledged that their own abilities, knowledge and strength were not enough, He meets them in the moment and fills their nets.

Truth #2: It is Jesus Who fills our nets. When we take the time to **wait** and **listen,** to depend on His direction in life, He makes life work for us. Jesus wants to work while we wait, to work in our circumstances. We tend to make decision after decision based on what we think we need to be happy. Jesus says, *"**Wait** and **listen** to Me, and I will tell you what you need to do to be happy."* We may only be a boat-width from the truth – but a boat-width is the difference between success and yet another failure.

- ✳ Are you looking for a potential spouse? ***Ask Jesus.***
- ✳ Are you deciding whether to change jobs? ***Ask Jesus.***

* Are you thinking about moving? ***Ask Jesus.***
* Are you going through a divorce? ***Ask Jesus.*** **Listen and wait.**
* Are you at any big crossroads in life? ***Ask Jesus.***

Jesus has something He wants us to do, something much more significant than catching fish. But if we are too busy throwing our nets in the water, we may miss Him. So stop, take some time to wait and seek Him, and listen. He wants to fill our nets.

Day 98: The Master Chef

John 21:7-14

Jesus Loves ALL IN

We just have to love Peter! I mean, as much as he messed up, he also is the most passionate and "ALL IN" of the disciples. I think Jesus really loved that about Peter, and that is why Jesus used Peter to establish the Church. As much as Peter made a mess of things, at least he was ALL IN. Jesus is looking for people who are ALL IN. Peter loved Jesus so much that when he heard it was the Lord on shore, he jumped in the water and headed straight for Him. The boat was too slow. Of course it was: it was filled with fish!

> Then the disciple Jesus loved said to Peter, "It's the Lord!" When Simon Peter heard that it was the Lord, he put on his tunic (for he had stripped for work), jumped into the water, and headed to shore. The others stayed with the boat, and pulled the loaded net to the shore for they were only about a hundred yards from shore.
>
> When they got there, they found breakfast waiting for them - fish cooked over a charcoal fire and some bread. "Bring some of the fish you've just caught," Jesus said. So Simon Peter went aboard and dragged the net to the shore. There were 153 large fish, and

yet the net hadn't torn. "Now come and have some breakfast!" Jesus said.

None of the disciples dared to ask Him, "Who are You?" They knew it was the Lord. Then Jesus served them the bread and the fish. This was the third time Jesus had appeared to His disciples since He had been raised from the dead.

John 21:7-14

I find it encouraging that Jesus cared about the fact that His disciples were hungry and cold. They had been out all night fishing, and hadn't eaten. Maybe there was a bit of "rust on their game" of professional fishing. So God starts a fire and cooks His friends some breakfast.

I just love the fact that God knows how to work the barbecue! Don't you just love this picture? God takes the time to start a fire and cook fish. Ever wonder how He started the fire? Did He call down fire from Heaven? Did He just touch the coals with His finger ... and "poof!"? Did He actually take the time to strike some tinder to start the fire? Or did He just think: "Fire" ... and there it was?

And isn't it very cool that God used some of the fish they had just caught? God wants to use what we bring to Him; He wants to use what we have to offer. He wants us to be a part of the solution.

Jesus was about to have a heavy conversation with His disciples, but He wanted to care for them first. He wanted to be sure they were warmed and filled. Even though He was now in His transformed body and in no need of food, He still was cognizant of His friends' human needs and cared that they were hungry. God knows our needs and cares about us. That makes me feel good.

Day 99: *"Three Times"*

John 21:15-17

Loving People

"By the time the rooster crows, you will have denied Me three times." Remember these words? Peter was asked three times in the courtyard – while Jesus was being held captive – if he knew Jesus. Three times Peter denied knowing his Lord and Friend. It was a public denial, and now Jesus was giving Peter a chance to make a public confession, to publicly confess his love for Jesus and close the loop on his sin of denial. By letting Peter affirm his love, Jesus was building courage back into the man and preparing him for the day he would go public with his faith ... and thousands would receive Christ. Here is how it went down.

> After breakfast, Jesus asked Simon Peter, "Simon, son of John, do you love Me more than these?"
>
> "Yes, Lord," Peter replied. "You know I love You."
>
> "Then feed My lambs," Jesus told him. Jesus repeated the question, "Simon, son of John, do you love Me?"
>
> "Yes, Lord," Peter said, "You know I love You!"

"Then take care of My sheep," Jesus said. A third time he asked him, "Simon, son of John, do you love Me?"

Peter was hurt that Jesus asked the question a third time. He said, "Lord, You know everything. You know that I love You."

Jesus said, "Then feed My sheep."

John 21:15-17

Three times Jesus asked Peter to confess his love. The first time, Jesus asked Peter if he loved him more than the other disciples; Peter said yes. Jesus knew that He was going to be requiring all from Peter, so He was establishing that Peter was indeed ready to give all.

Here we see how Jesus wants us to love Him: **by loving and caring for other believers.** It comes back to the great commandment Jesus gave: *"Love God, and love your neighbor."* We prove our love for Jesus by acting on our love for others. Jesus said, *"The world will know you are Mine by your love for one another."*

Jesus asks a second time, and when Peter says, *"Yes, Lord, you know I love You"* – Jesus tells him to act out this love by taking care of His sheep. His sheep would be the Jews who would come to salvation through Peter's confession and ministry.

Here Jesus is saying to Peter, *"Not only do I want you to catch fish but I want you to clean them. I want you not to just evangelize people but shepherd them once they become My sheep."*

Then a third time, to really cement this into Peter's soul, Jesus gave him one more opportunity to publicly proclaim his love for his Savior. A third time, Jesus was saying, *"If you really love Me, then spend your life taking care of and feeding My sheep, My Church."*

It is really worth noting that to love Jesus **is** to love His sheep. One might ask, *"How do I go about loving someone I cannot see, touch or feel?"* The answer is we act out our love for Jesus by pouring out love on His Body: each believer. By feeding His lambs. By feeding His sheep.

Each of us can love Jesus well by coming alongside His children and helping them in their walk with Christ. This can be done by teaching kids in church, helping in the nursery, becoming part of a small group, loving and serving other believers in the Church. Jesus loves it when we love Him by loving His little lambs and His sheep.

Do you want to love Jesus well? Love His sheep well.

Day 100: *"Follow Me"*

John 21:18-22

Become Eternally-Minded

Jesus freely gave Himself on the cross, and we freely receive His gift of forgiveness for our sins and Eternal Life with Him. However, there is a cost to identifying and living with Christ.

Once we become Eternally-minded, we no longer live for this world and what it offers. There is a cost to following Christ, and Jesus foretold to Peter that it would cost him his very life.

> "I tell you the truth: when you were young, you were able to do as you liked; you dressed yourself and went wherever you wanted to go. But when you are old, you will stretch out your hands, and others will dress you and take you where you don't want to go." Jesus said this to let him know by what kind of death he would glorify God. Then Jesus told him, "Follow Me."
>
> Peter turned around and saw behind them the disciple Jesus loved - the one who had leaned over to Jesus during supper and asked, "Lord, who will betray You?"
>
> Peter asked Jesus, "What about him, Lord?"

John 21:18-21

Do you ever compare your life with someone else's life, and ask God, *"Why aren't they suffering like I am?"* or *"Why do they have it so good?"*

Peter was saying, *"Well, if I have to die for You, then what about John? You are always favoring him, Lord. You pay special attention to him, he always gets to sit next to You. If I have to die a painful death, at least let me know I am not alone!"* We tend to compare our lives and circumstances to others, but Jesus simply wants us to keep our eyes on Him, trust Him and not worry about how He works with others.

> Jesus replied, "If I want him to remain alive until I return, what is that to you? As for you, follow Me."
>
> **John 21:22**

Jesus simply says, ***"Follow Me."*** Do not worry about others. Jesus was not saying that John would somehow miraculously live forever. We know John ended up in exile on the Isle of Patmos, where he received the revelation of Jesus Christ and wrote down the vision that would become the book of Revelation. Each of us is responsible to Jesus for our own response to Him, and how well we follow Him. He wants us to keep our eyes and attention on Him, not on any other person. Sometimes we get our eyes on a great Christian leader or teacher, and then if they fall, we find ourselves disenchanted and distrusting.

Jesus will never fall, He will never fail, He will never disappoint us. We need to keep our eyes on Him because He is faithful and true.

"As for you, follow Me."

Day 101: We Believe!

John 21:24-25

Eye-Witnesses

In a Court of Law, it only takes one reputable witness to tell the truth under oath so that a jury of twelve peers can return an accurate verdict. John was just one of hundreds of witnesses to Jesus' life, death and resurrection.

These men who lived with Jesus and wrote about Jesus were not only eye-witnesses to His life, but put their own lives at risk by identifying with Jesus. In fact, every one of them eventually were put to death for their affiliation with Jesus of Nazareth. Historically, Jesus' life, death and resurrection had more eye-witness proof than most accounts we hear of happening, even in our own day.

> This disciple is the one who testifies to these events and has recorded them here. And we know that his account of these things is accurate. Jesus also did many other things. If they were all written down, I supposed the whole world could not contain the books that would be written.
>
> **John 21:24-25**

What a journey we have had through the Book of John! Thank you for joining me on this fulfilling and deepening adventure. God's Word is amazing and so full of life – my heart has been forever impacted by these 101 days.

Remember: God's Word is true, it is accurate. The most important things we have learned from John are: Jesus is the eternal God, came to Earth as a human ... the Lamb of God to take away the sins of the world ... the Word of the Father, lived, loved, died, rose, and reigns forever. He is our Savior, Friend, Redeemer, and King.

We believe in God the Father
Almighty, Maker of Heaven
and Earth
And in Jesus Christ, His only
begotten Son, our Lord
Who was conceived by the Holy
Spirit, born of the virgin Mary
Suffered under Pontius Pilate,
was crucified, dead and buried
He descended into Hell
The third day, He rose again
from the dead
He ascended in Heaven, and sits
at the right hand of God the
Father Almighty
From hence He shall come to
judge the living and the dead

We believe in the Holy Spirit
We believe in the holy Church of
Christ, cleansed by His blood
We believe in the communion of
the saints, the forgiveness of sin
The resurrection of the body, and
Life Everlasting.
Amen.

Recommended Resources

Wiersbe, Warren W.: *The Bible Exposition Commentary.* Wheaton, Ill. : Victor Books, 1996, c1989, S. Jn 4:1

Acknowledgements

There are many people who contributed wisdom and inspiration, and helped make this book happen. These are people I've worked with who believed in me, took a risk and invested in me:

- **Dr. Kim Ryan,** Senior Pastor, *North County Christ the King Church,* Lynden, Washington; from 2003 to the present
- **Ralph Bressler,** Principal, *Morrison Academy,* Taichung, Taiwan; from 2001 to 2003
- **Dr. Jim Hayford,** *Eastside Foursquare Church,*
- Bothell, Washington; from 1996 to 2001
- **Pastor Larry Wersen,** *His Place Community Church,* Burlington, Washington; from 1984 to 1996.
- **Jeanne Halsey,** who encouraged me to take the leap into the abyss of publishing.
- To all the friends who have woven their unique and beautiful threads into the fabric of my life.

Dedication

To **Gwen, Levi** and **Lindsey** – my family, whom I dearly love, who have lived with me in this glass house of pastoral ministry.

To **Wilbur Langstraat,** father, who modeled what it means to love God's Word.

To **Wilma Langstraat,** my mother, who read to me and passed on to me a love for literature and creative writing.

About the Author

Kurt Langstraat has been in pastoral ministry for 25 years as youth pastor, worship leader and currently associate pastor in Marriage and Family Ministries. He and his wife Gwen are parents of two adult children, Levi and Lindsey. Kurt currently serves on the staff at *North County Christ the King Church* in Lynden, Washington, U.S.A. His work includes overseeing Men's Ministry, Marriage Ministry, Children's Ministry, and seeing people for life coaching and teaching when needed.

About this book, Kurt says: *"I never intended to write a book; I'm far too busy. However, a couple of years ago I did an online interactive devotional through the Book of John. It started out as a way to connect with my son Levi as he was away at Washington State University. Every day I would get up about 5:00am and read a section of John, make some comments, and post it on Facebook. At the end of 101 days, I completed John, and had gathered a small crowd of people who loved it.*

"One of those people was Jeanne Halsey, who is a professional ghost writer. She collected all the postings, compiled it into a book format, printed off

a copy, and handed it to me on my 50th birthday. She said, 'This is good enough to be published." So, Jeanne, I blame you for all this.

"I dedicate this work to the ones God has given me to love dearly: my wife Gwen, my son Levi, and my daughter Lindsey. May you come to know God better as you read these reflections on the Book of John."

About The Editor

Jeanne Halsey is an accomplished writer, having worked for Christian ministries and secular individuals for over 30 years, and ghostwriting dozens of books, articles and commentaries. She has published many books under her own byline; she also enjoys teaching *The School of Creative Christian Writing,* helping others unlock their God-given gift of writing.

Regarding *GOD 101*, she says: *"It has been a treat to help Kurt write and finish his first published book. When I transferred Kurt's raw file over to my computer to format and edit for publication, his original cut-and-paste Bible verses became 'technically corrupted,' meaning I was required to type in all the Bible verses myself. Which meant that by the time I reached the end of 101 devotionals, I had written out the entire Book of*

John. Wow, I have 'God's Word Power' surging through my veins!"

Jeanne and her husband Kenneth Halsey live in Blaine, Washington; they have two married children and five grandchildren. The Halseys are active members of *North County Christ the King Community Church* in Lynden, Washington. Jeanne can be reached at: www.halseywrite.com or go to www.lulu.com to order her books.

GOD101